CLINICAL AND OBSERVATIONAL PSYCHOANALYTIC RESEARCH

Monograph Series of

The Psychoanalysis Unit of University College London

and

The Anna Freud Centre

Series Editors

Joseph Sandler & Peter Fonagy

1 J. Sandler, A. Holder, C. Dare, & A. U. Dreher, *Freud's Models of the Mind: An Introduction*

2 J. Sandler & P. Fonagy, *Recovered Memories of Abuse: True or False?*

3 A. Hurry, *Psychoanalysis and Developmental Therapy*

4 A. U. Dreher, *Foundations for Conceptual Research in Psychoanalysis*

PSYCHOANALYTIC MONOGRAPHS

No. 5

CLINICAL AND OBSERVATIONAL PSYCHOANALYTIC RESEARCH: ROOTS OF A CONTROVERSY

edited by

Joseph Sandler, Anne-Marie Sandler, & Rosemary Davies

contributors

André Green & Daniel N. Stern

with

Anne Alvarez *Irma Brenman Pick*

Rosine Jozef Perelberg *Robert S. Wallerstein*

Introduction by

Riccardo Steiner

Routledge
Taylor & Francis Group
LONDON AND NEW YORK

First published 2000 by Karnac Books Ltd.

Published 2019 by Routledge
2 Park Square, Milton Park, Abingdon, Oxon OX14 4RN
52 Vanderbilt Avenue, New York, NY 10017

First issued in hardback 2019

Routledge is an imprint of the Taylor & Francis Group, an informa business

British Library Cataloguing in Publication Data
A C.I.P. for this book is available from the British Library

ISBN 13: 978-0-367-10506-8 (hbk)
ISBN 13: 978-1-85575-229-0 (pbk)

THE PSYCHOANALYSIS UNIT AT UNIVERSITY COLLEGE LONDON was founded by Joseph Sandler in 1984, when he was appointed to the Freud Memorial Chair of Psychoanalysis in the University of London (which replaced the annual Freud Memorial Visiting Professorship at UCL). The Unit is based in the Psychology Department, arguably the strongest, and certainly the broadest, department of psychology in the United Kingdom. The Unit quickly became a thriving centre for academic psychoanalysis and established a busy doctoral programme in psychoanalytic research. A weekly programme of lectures was organized, and several highly successful psychoanalytic conferences have been held each year. Through the Unit psychoanalysis began to occupy a central place in the intellectual life of University College London.

The Unit initiated close collaboration with the International Psychoanalytical Association. Major scientific meetings of the Association were held in conjunction with the Unit, including the annual IPA Conference in Psychoanalytic Research and an IPA Conference on Psychoanalysis and Literature. In addition to fostering these important links between international psychoanalysis and the British university, the Unit maintains close ties with the British Psycho-Analytical Society. It collaborates regularly with the major theoretical groups within the Society in offering an academic platform for presenting and discussing their views.

In 1992 Peter Fonagy succeeded Joseph Sandler in the Freud Chair, with Professor Sandler remaining as a Co-director of the Unit. The Unit's focus on post-graduate education has continued, with now over a dozen Ph.D. students at any one time. In collaboration with the British Psycho-Analytical Society, the Unit has created a Master of Science degree in Theoretical Psychoanalytic Studies (non-clinical). Over the years, the strength of the link between the Unit and other psychoanalytic organizations has increased, with academic members of the staff of The Anna Freud Centre becoming affiliated to the University via the Psychoanalysis Unit. The Unit's original links to the Psychology Department have been maintained and developed, with Professor Fonagy assuming the headship of the Sub-Department of Clinical Health Psychology on its inception in 1994. The international influence of the Unit continues to increase, and in 1995 it organized and hosted the first research training programme for psychoanalysts sponsored by the International Psycho-Analytical Association. As part of this development, leading psychoanalytic researchers became visiting professors of the Unit; these have included Professors Robert Emde, Horst Kächele, Wilma Bucci, Otto Kernberg, and Peter Hobson.

The mission of the Unit remains the integration of psychoanalytic ideas with academic pursuits across a range of disciplines—literature, medicine, the social sciences, the arts. The Unit frequently consults with leading academics from those disciplines who seek advice on psychoanalytic aspects of their work. It has become a national and international centre for psychoanalytic research and scholarship.

THE ANNA FREUD CENTRE was founded by Anna Freud in 1940 as the Hampstead War Nurseries, which provided a home for children who had lost their own homes or were separated from their parents in some other way in the Blitz. After the war, Anna Freud responded to the urgent demand for greater expertise in child mental health and the childhood disorders by founding The Hampstead Child Therapy Course and the Clinic, which, after Anna Freud's death, was renamed in 1984 as The Anna Freud Centre.

Since its inception, The Hampstead Child Therapy Course has provided high-level, intensive training in all aspects of child psychoanalysis and psychotherapy. Training at the Centre has received formal accreditation from the International Association for Child Psychoanalysis, and many of the child psychoanalysts and psychotherapists trained at the Centre are currently practicing in the United Kingdom and elsewhere.

After the untimely death in 1992 of the Director, George Moran, Rose Edgcumbe functioned as Acting Director until 1993, when Anne-Marie Sandler was appointed to the Directorship. After her retirement in 1996, Julia Fabricius was appointed to the post. In addition to combining therapy, training, and research, the Centre provides a psychiatric assessment and advisory service for children and young adults, long-term therapy and young adults' consultation and preventive services, and an internationally recognized and highly esteemed programme of research. In an important collaboration with University College London, the Centre offers a Master of Science degree in Psychoanalytic Developmental Psychology. This unique course reflects the extension and accreditation of the Centre's well-established teaching programme.

PUBLISHER'S NOTE

Joseph Sandler, 1927–1998

It was very much in keeping with Joseph Sandler's character to select a possibly controversial topic of prime relevance and then to organize a forum for its debate amongst the leading scholars on opposite sides of the argument. This method of stimulating continuous progress and dialogue in psychoanalysis can be seen, for instance, in the 1986 conference that Joe organized during his tenure as Sigmund Freud Professor of Psychoanalysis at the Hebrew University of Jerusalem, on which the volume *Projection, Identification, Projective Identification* (1988) was based. Another example of this kind was the conference held in June 1994 at University College London on recovered memories of abuse. This conference produced the material that Joe, together with Peter Fonagy, edited as *Recovered Memories of Abuse* (1997).

The present volume on the debate on infant research in psychoanalysis is the last one on which I had the privilege to work with Joe. His untimely death on the 6th of October 1998 did not allow him to complete the editing or to write an Introduction. In the discussion section in part II, though, there is an intervention of Joe's that typifies his gifts: it is a little gem, clarifying the concept of the unconscious in relation to references made by other contributors. It is a fitting tribute to Joe that this book was completed, thanks above all to Anne-Marie Sandler and Peter Fonagy and to the highly professional editing of Rosemary Davies. All of the contributors have shown great forbearance, and in particular André Green has generously helped in adjusting his contributions from the verbal to the written form. Riccardo Steiner has stepped in for Joe by writing the Introduction. In his unique way, he makes palpable the respect and affection that united the two of them despite their sometimes differing views on psychoanalysis.

I had the good fortune not only to work with Joe—a very special and rewarding experience—but also to count him as a mentor and a good friend. He was always ready to listen to and value opinions on the subject of which he was a master, even from a layman such as myself. Riccardo, with his particular insight, once identified the kind of scholarship characteristic of Joe as that of the Talmudic tradition. Joe's intellectual rigour and integrity are a legacy that hopefully will stay with us not as a set of rigid rules, but as I believe he would wish: that we should have an open mind ready to listen to all sides of an argument within its historical development.

Cesare Sacerdoti

CONTENTS

PUBLISHER'S NOTE ix

EDITORS AND CONTRIBUTORS xiii

PREFACE xvii

Introduction
Riccardo Steiner 1

PART ONE

1 What kind of research for psychoanalysis?
André Green 21

2 Psychoanalytic research: where do we disagree?
Robert S. Wallerstein 27

3 Response to Robert S. Wallerstein
André Green 32

PART TWO

4 Science and science fiction in infant research
André Green 41

5 The relevance of empirical infant research to psychoanalytic theory and practice
Daniel N. Stern 73

6 Discussion (I)
Rosine Jozef Perelberg 91

7 Discussion (II)
Anne Alvarez 100

8 Discussion (III)
Irma Brenman Pick 108

9 Plenary discussion 119

REFERENCES 143

INDEX 155

EDITORS AND CONTRIBUTORS

Anne Alvarez, PhD, is a Consultant Child and Adolescent Psychotherapist and Co-Convener of the Autism Service, Child and Family Department, Tavistock Clinic, London. She is also a Consultant to a research project at the University of Pisa, on Mother–Infant Psychotherapy with Toddlers with Pervasive Developmental Disorder. She has published many papers on psychoanalytic psychotherapy with autistic, borderline, and traumatized patients and is the author of *Live Company: Psychotherapy with Autistic, Borderline, Deprived and Abused Children* (1992) and edited, with Susan Reid, *Autism and Personality: Findings from the Tavistock Autism Workshop* (1999). A book of her seminars at the Brazilian Psychoanalytic Society, *Anne Alvarez in Sao Paulo,* was published in 1999.

André Green is a Training Analyst for the Paris Psychoanalytic Society where he has also been the former President and Director of the Paris Psychoanalytic Institute. He was also Vice President of the International Psychoanalytical Society and Professor of University College London, for the Freud Memorial Chair. Presently he is an Honorary Professor at the Buenos Aires University, a Member of the Moscow Academy of Humanities Research, and a Member of the New York Academy of Sciences. He has written numerous articles and books, some of which have been published in English, including *On Private Madness* (1986); *The Work of the Negative* (1999); *The Dead Mother—The Work of André Green* (1999); *The Fabric of Affect in the Psychoanalytic Discourse* (1999); and *André Green at The Squiggle Foundation* (2000).

Rosemary Davies is a Member of the British Psycho-Analytical Society. She works in private practice and in the National Health Service. She is a member of the Young Adults Research Project at The Anna Freud Centre.

Rosine Jozef Perelberg is a Training Analyst at the British Psycho-Analytical Society. She gained her doctorate in Social Anthropology at the London School of Economics, London. For the last ten years she has been a member of the Young Adults Research Project at The Anna Freud Centre, and she is also in private practice. She has edited *Gender and Power in Families* (with Anne Miller, 1990); *Female Experience: Three Generations of British Woman Psychoanalysts on Work with Women* (with Joan Raphael-Leff, 1997); and *Psychoanalytic Understanding of Violence and Suicide* (1998).

Irma Brenman Pick has an Honours degree in Social Sciences from the University of Witwatersrand. In London, she trained first as a child psychotherapist at the Tavistock Clinic and later as an adult and child analyst at the British Institute of Psychoanalysis. She is a training analyst, a Past Chairman of the Education Committee, and also Past Chairman of the International Psychoanalytical Association Committee on Psychoanalytic Education. She is recent Past President of the British Psycho-Analytical Society. Her papers published in the *International Journal of Psycho-Analysis* include "Adolescence: Its Impact on Patient and Analyst", "Working Through in the Counter Transference", and, most recently, "Concern: Spurious and Real".

Anne-Marie Sandler studied with Jean Piaget in Geneva and was for a time his assistant. She then came to England, where she trained in child analysis with Anna Freud, going on to complete the adult training in the British Psycho-Analytical Society, where she is a training and supervising analyst. She has been President of the British Society and of the European Psychoanalytical Federation, and Vice-President of the International Psychoanalytical Association. She was formerly Director of the Anna Freud Centre. Many of her published papers were written in collaboration with Joseph Sandler. They also collaborated on a book, *Internal Objects Revisited*, published in 1998.

Joseph Sandler was born in Cape Town, South Africa. He did his doctoral research in psychology at the Institute of Psychiatry, London. Subsequently he pursued medical studies at University College London. He was a training analyst at the British Psychoanalytical Society and Past President of the International Psychoanalytical Association and of the European Psychoanalytical Federation. He has been Editor-in-Chief of the *British Journal of Medical Psychology*, the *International Journal of Psychoanalysis*, and the *International Review of Psycho-Analysis*. He published numerous papers and books on psychoanalysis and allied topics and was awarded the Sigourney Award for outstanding contributions to psychoanalysis.

Riccardo Steiner is a member of the British Psychoanalytic Association and is in private practice.

Daniel Stern is currently Professeur Ordinaire in the Faculté de Psychologie, Université de Genève, Switzerland; Adjunct Professor in the Department of Psychiatrie, Cornell University Medical School, New York Hospital; and a Lecturer at the Columbia University Center for Psychoanalysis. He received his training at Harvard University in 1956; at Albert Einstein College of Medicine, 1960; at Bellevue Hospital, New York, 1962; at The National Institute of Health, 1964; and at Columbia University, 1967, 1972. He is the author of five books, most of which have been translated into several languages: *The First Relationship: Infant and Mother* (1977); *The Interpersonal World of the Infant: A View from Psychoanalysis and Developmental Psychology* (1985); *The Journal of a Baby* (1990); *The Motherhood Constellation: A Unifying View of Parent-In-*

fant Psychotherapies (1995); and, with Nadia Bruschweiler-Stern, *The Birth of a Mother* (1997).

Robert Wallerstein is Professor Emeritus and former Chair, Department of Psychiatry, University of California San Francisco School of Medicine, and Training and Supervising Analyst, San Francisco Psychoanalytic Institute. He is Past President of the International Psychoanalytical Association (1985–89) and of the American Psychoanalytic Association (1971–72). He has published numerous papers and books in the field of psychoanalysis, including *Forty-two Lives in Treatment: A Study of Psychoanalysis and Psychotherapy* (1986) and *The Talking Cures: The Psychoanalyses and the Psychotherapies* (1995).

PREFACE

In March of this year, Peter Fonagy and Ron Britton delivered papers at the Institute of Psychoanalysis in London debating the vexed question of psychoanalysis and research. The title of their presentation, "Psychoanalysis and Research: Grasping the Nettle", reminds us of the controversial and difficult challenges for psychoanalysis posed by present-day notions of research evidence and the scientific method.

A conference on just this topic, chaired by Joseph Sandler, was hosted by University College London (UCL) in September 1997. At that conference—as Cesare Sacerdoti and Riccardo Steiner separately describe herein—the nettle was indeed grasped, and a heated debate ensued. The edited proceedings of that conference are reproduced here in part II; a preliminary debate that was first published in the *International Psychoanalytical Association Newsletter* is presented in part I.

We would like to thank all the contributors for risking the stinging encounter, and for their patience during the transition into print. Our thanks go also to Paula Barkay, who skilfully organized the very successful UCL conference, which was attended by over two hundred people. We thank her and Kathy Leach for their help in the editing process: their good-natured and thoughtful assistance has been invaluable. And we are indebted to Eric and Klara King for their excellent editing and preparation of the manuscript for publication.

* * *

The book is dedicated to the memory of Joe Sandler. We hope he would have regarded this as a fitting completion of the work he began.

Rosemary Davies and Anne-Marie Sandler
May 2000

CLINICAL AND OBSERVATIONAL PSYCHOANALYTIC RESEARCH

Introduction

Riccardo Steiner

> Psychoanalytic investigation reaching back into childhood from a later time and contemporary observation of children, combine to indicate to us still other regularly active sources of sexual excitation. The direct observation of children has the disadvantage of working upon data which are easily misunderstandable. Psychoanalysis is made difficult by the fact that it can only reach its data as well as its conclusions after long detours. But by cooperation the two methods can attain a satisfactory degree of certainty in their finding. [Freud, *Three Essays on the Theory of Sexuality*, 1905d, p. 201]

I do not know whether by quoting those conciliatory statements somebody would have been able to calm the at times rather turbulent waters of the meeting between André Green and Daniel Stern, held at University College London, on 1 November 1997, under the chairmanship of Joseph Sandler. Anne Alvarez, Rosine Perelberg, and Irma Brenman Pick were the discussants of the papers of the two main speakers.

But there is no doubt that the wish to discuss and evaluate the pros and cons of what Freud called the "cooperation of the two methods" was the main reason that lay behind organizing such a meeting.

As Green and Stern remind us, it was not the first time that they had met in public—arousing the same interest and turbulence—to comment on and to criticize each other's viewpoints on the relevance of baby observation to psychoanalysis. Yet we must be truly grateful to the subtle, containing, dialogic skills of Joseph Sandler that the reader now has at his or her disposal such rich and lively food for thought. Sandler worked at the editing of this book even during the last months of his life, bringing it nearly to the point of completion, and that has made his effort even more moving. His work has been completed with affectionate care by Anne-Marie Sandler and Rosemary Davies and is published in this series, which is to be edited henceforth by Peter Fonagy and Anne-Marie Sandler.[1] Joseph Sandler deliberately tried to edit even many of the interventions from the audience at the meeting. That, besides giving the reader a more direct experience of the atmosphere and the issues discussed, has also preserved between the lines Sandler's voice and contributions: his legendary talmudic ability to chisel and to clarify details and, in particular, fundamental conceptual issues, but overall, in this case, his patient, facilitating irony. He had to make good use of it to chair this meeting. Indeed, one could say that—particularly for those who remember some of the exchanges between Green, Stern, and also the audience—instead of a meeting, at times it was an unforgettable confrontation. That is the reason why I have referred to it as turbulent!

Yet this was not only due to the different personalities of the main speakers or to their personal idiosyncrasies. Indeed, the two main papers, together with the interventions of the discussants and their differences in supporting either Green's or Stern's views—more in line with Green's views, the intervention of Irma Brenman Pick, although she has a different attitude to baby observation from that of Green; more in favour of Stern, Anne Alvarez, who is very keen on using data coming from Stern and other researchers in her

[1] I have been touched by Cesare Sacerdoti's proposal that I should write this Introduction and by the fact that Anne-Marie Sandler and Peter Fonagy have accepted it. I would also like to thank Joan Raphael-Leff and Mary Target for their bibliographic help.

clinical work; more balanced, that of Rosine Perelberg, who nevertheless introduced a very interesting viewpoint, based also on her anthropological background—all this, as I said, allows the reader to become acquainted with some of the major critical issues that characterize, for good and for ill, contemporary psychoanalysis in many of its aspects. This is also evident if the reader looks at the interventions from the audience at the meeting.

To understand all those issues better, the reader should, of course, refer to the complete works of André Green and of Daniel Stern, bearing in mind that even as far as Green's views on baby observation are concerned, some of his most important theoretical contributions are not available in English.[2]

One of the possible ways to try to make sense of the reasons why the main speakers, but also all the participants, presented such interesting different viewpoints is to be aware that they reflected, besides different personalities, at least two different "cultures" and ways of understanding and interpreting "psychoanalysis"[3] and what it is to be a psychoanalyst today, when confronted with how to evaluate and to use empirical research and not only that coming from what is called systematic and scientific baby observation.

From one side, one could say that with regard to Green's paper we have a particularly French way of understanding all those issues, and, from the other, with regard to Stern's, the Anglo–American way of looking at all this—although, just thinking about some of the statements in Brenman Pick's intervention, one has to be careful not to identify the whole Anglo–American psychoanalytic culture under the same umbrella! This is the reason why I used the expression "at least two cultures".

To remind the reader of some of those differences, just think of Green's complex and passionate polemical paper—his rigorous anti-scientist and anti-objectivistic attitude, his uncompromising

[2] See, for instance, the very important and illuminating "À propos de l'observation des bébés" (Green, 1992), based on an interview with Green by P. Geissmann. However, a number of his other works have recently been published in English: see Green (1999a, 1999b) and Kohon (1999); see also Abram (2000).

[3] Perelberg made this point in her intervention. See also Steiner (1984, 1987) and Wallerstein (1988).

defence of Freud's clinical and metapsychological views, particularly his theory of drives and his notion of the "unconscious" as expressed even in his later work, for instance in *The Ego and the Id* (1923d). During the last four decades, Green has written some of the most intelligent and thought-provoking interpretations of Freud's later work. Or just think of Green's insistence, in the name of what he calls "the psychoanalytic state of mind", on his personal interpretation of Freud's *Nachträglichkeit*, which in English has been translated in a rather misleading way as "deferred action" and in French as *"après coup"*. According to Green, this does not allow for any notion or event experienced in "the here and now" of the life of the infant, in whatever form, which can be preserved or described as such and which can be meaningful from the psychoanalytic viewpoint as he understands it. Because, by definition, according to Green we can only reconstruct those events *post factum* with all the complications, distortions, unconscious processes and defences, and personal projections of the adult observer or interpreter or narrator of those events. This viewpoint is at the core of Green's disagreement with Stern and other researchers. Furthermore, recall Green's adamant defence of the psychoanalytic notion of "intrapsychic" and of the model of psychic reality based on unconscious conflicts and on the dream and its processes, as opposed to Stern's and others' notion of "observable interaction" or "interpersonal relationship" between the infant and the mother. Remember also Green's insistence on the importance of sexuality in the psychic reality of the baby and the role played by affects and the way that Green understands them. Of great importance to clarifying his viewpoint is also his extremely sophisticated interpretation of Freud's notion of temporality and primary narcissism and his constant reference to the clinical setting as the only real "place" where rigorous psychoanalysis can get its "knowledge", not so much about the "real" infant as about "the infantile", which is in all of us but only reachable through the free associations and interpretations of the patient and the analyst, where language and the constant reference to the triangular situation represented by the Oedipus complex are of fundamental and unique importance. Although Green does not deny their value as observations for psychological research, he is convinced that there is no real value for psychoanalysis, as far as the "intrapsychic life" is concerned, in any systematic so-called objective observational study of babies or infants, to the point that he defines them as science fiction as far as their so-called scientific rigour is concerned. He also denies any heuristic value to any other kind of empirically based developmental research in psychoanalysis. And that is the reason in this paper for his polemic not only against Stern but also against Emde, Fonagy, and other researchers. According to him, all this is in danger of destroying the specificity of psychoanalysis and its methods or leads to enormous simplifications.

Green cannot accept Stern's views, even when Stern tries to use, in his own way, Green's clinical material, particularly his paper "The Dead Mother" (1986a).[4] Of course, one could go on concentrating on other specific aspects of Green's paper. What I think the reader should also consider, however, are Green's expressive rhetorical devices and the encompassing complexity of his paper, which is focused not just on Stern's work. At times one is reminded of a solitary, worried biblical prophet, warrior, and defender of Freud's work as he understands it, not so much to stick dogmatically to it, but to remind everybody, particularly at this moment in history, of the danger of forgetting the richness and still unsurpassed complexity of Freud's inspirational model, if one wants to remain loyal to what Green feels and means by psychoanalysis. Uncompromising polarizations of viewpoints are often what characterize Green's style and way of communicating. But there is no doubt that whatever the reader can make of Green's way of thinking, his particular manner of reading and interpreting Freud can only be fully appreciated, as I have already mentioned, if one refers to the French cultural tradition that lies behind this approach to psychoanalysis—and at least partially to the influence of Lacan, although Green has been open, as this paper also bears witness, to all sorts of other influences, such as those of Klein, Bion, Rosenfeld, Searles, and especially Winnicott.

Particularly influential is Lacan's at times brilliant reinterpretation of Freud's concepts such as that of *Nachträglichkeit* and of *Trieb* as opposed to instinct,[5] and his polemic attitude towards what he

---

[4] See for instance, Stern (1995b), p. 99.

[5] *Trieb* in English has been translated as "drive" and in French as "*pulsion*". "Drive" and "*pulsion*" have slightly different meanings.

thought was already a behaviouristic, biologistic adaptational and reductionistic psychologization of psychoanalysis, coming from American ego psychology and its scientist empirical ramifications during the 1950s. But one should also remember Lacan's rather polemic attitude towards the British school of object relations and, in spite of his genuine admiration for Melanie Klein's work, his criticism of the exclusive importance that, according to him, Klein gave to the early object relationship between the baby and the mother. Echoes of this criticism are undoubtedly present even in Green's attitude towards psychoanalytically oriented baby observation, like that derived from Esther Bick. It is not by chance that baby observation forms no part of the training curriculum of either of the French psychoanalytic societies belonging to the I.P.A.

Consider now, by contrast, some of the issues present in the much more restricted and focused paper by Daniel Stern—his gentle firmness in defending his own point of view, which he claims is, although indirectly, useful to psychoanalysis; his conviction, in the name of a pluralistic, empirical approach, to be speaking not without the walls of an embattled psychoanalysis, as according to Green, but from within. Just think also of Stern's insistence on the preverbal, non-verbal interaction and particularly on the *observable, a-conflictual communication* between the mother and the baby—something that Stern is also so able to communicate when he speaks, to the point that the written version of his paper seems lacking in something semiotically very important: his capacity for mimicry and ability to "act" his brilliant observations in front of the audience, using his voice, gestures, and body movements. It is not by chance that in trying to explain how he came to his results and how he created his research's methodology, Stern refers in his paper to the work he did with dancers and theatrical performers, who in order to express themselves and to communicate with the audience have to rely not so much on words but on their body language. There is perhaps an important theoretical issue that all this raises, if one thinks even further of the extremely subtle attempt that Stern makes to convey and to explain the lived experience and interaction between the baby and the mother from the point of view of the perceiving baby, in what Stern calls "the coup", the here and now of the experienceable and of the observable; he uses music as the model via which he tries to explain how that happens and can be understood, and he refers to the way the melodic phrase is created. By definition, music is a language in itself, which does not need words to be communicated. In Stern, there is an insistence on the non-verbalizable, on the lived experience of the baby, which is not so dramatically affected by the *"aprés coup"* and can be retraced even later on: that is what makes his own observations and hypotheses valuable to psychoanalysis and to its clinical methodology, according to him.

Think by contrast of the importance that Green accords to language and to its importance for psychoanalysis in general, although the prosodic aspects of communication and the semiotic ones are very important too. After all, even Freud relied on theatre at one point to try to make sense of what he was discovering in himself and in "the infantile" of his patients. But what mattered most for him in Sophocles' *Oedipus Rex* or Shakespeare's *Hamlet* was, overall, the words linked to the *"unbewusste Phantasie"*, the unconscious phantasies, of Oedipus, his parents, Hamlet, and so on. Freud's interpretation of the infantile and its conflicts in Oedipus, Jocasta, Laius, Hamlet, and so forth relied on the dream and its processes and not so much on the observable aspects of their behaviour, although, of course, he took the descriptions by their authors into consideration too.

Beside the brilliant attempt that Stern makes to describe what he calls the "vitality contours" of the affective and cognitive lived experience of the baby, probably one of the most important points in his paper is where he tries to describe what we should imagine is a baby's experience of time. It is interesting that Stern refers to what was, according to him, Freud's notion of time, which he considers a chronological time, coming from the natural sciences and from physics in particular. Stern suggests a different, and according to him more appropriate and richer, way of looking at the experience of time in the baby, using a phenomenological descriptive approach that is extremely subtle and sophisticated, derived from Husserl and his notion of "intentionality". At the same time, nevertheless, one has to remember that Husserl's viewpoint was purely philosophical and against psychoanalysis and psychology in general and that his notion of intentionality, which he derived from Brentano, excludes by definition any reference to the unconscious. Perhaps that is one of the reasons why even in this paper Stern cannot make any use of Freud's notion of unconscious ego as expressed in Freud's *The Ego and the Id*, and his references to Freud's theory of the drives and their relationship to the unconscious are very vague. He insists on the commonsensical relationship between the baby and his mother. Brenman Pick objected to all this in her comments on Stern's paper, as of course did Green. There is also something else very interesting that, incidentally, shows the particular blending of Stern's culture, who, one should not forget, teaches also in Geneva and therefore has been open and receptive to all sorts of stimuli—among others, those of Piaget. Stern, in his work has come—as he also claims in his paper here—in his own way to the conclusion that together with an ego-centred attitude in the baby, there is an aspect of its way of relating which, since the earliest moments of its life, acknowledges the existence of the other, although in a very primitive way, something that—particularly in England—the followers of Klein, using her intuitions and hypotheses and observations, have claimed for more than half a century. But it is significant that in his paper Stern quotes Stein Braten but makes no reference at all to Klein. Her views concerning unconscious phantasies in the baby are far too speculative from an observable developmental point of view, based as they are not only on observable behaviour but overall interpsychic conflicts and on the role played by the drives, which Stern seems to consider too remote from his own approach.[6] The reader should also consider Stern's sophisticated defence of his method, his insistence on not being considered only a behaviourist, and particularly his statements concerning the kind of relevance, scientificity, and objectivity he is trying to reach with his systematic study of the baby. Stern insists that he is aiming not so much, as in the field of the natural sciences, at hypothesis testing but at hypothesis generating and that his researches are essential to establish what are unlikely and what are possible hypotheses in psychoanalysis from a developmental point of view.

---

[6] It might be of interest for the reader to consider that Stern's work has been critically studied by the Tavistock school of baby observation mainly inspired by Bick. See, for instance, *Closely Observed Infants* (Miller, Rustin, Rustin, & Shuttleworth, 1989). The Anna Freud Centre has, of course, been much more positively receptive to his views. See, for instance, *Psychoanalysis and Developmental Therapy* (Hurry, 1998).

Furthermore, his own receptiveness to so many different stimuli—from cognitivism, statistical studies, academic psychology, neurosciences, sophisticated techniques of observations (such as films), the arts, certain developments of philosophy—allows, according to him, psychoanalysis to be linked to the rest of our current knowledge. "When this relatedness is broken or becomes too weakened, the psychoanalytical discourse stops being interesting and gets left behind", he claims at one point.

There is no doubt at all in thinking that we are faced in the case of Stern with the typical pragmatic, rich, but at times rather eclectic open-mindedness of contemporary American culture, not just in the field of baby observations or psychoanalysis, which nevertheless in the United States has undergone an explosion that has led to all sorts of pluralistic avenues since the end of the 1960s.

Stern's fears that, without the help of empirical research even coming from developmental studies, psychoanalysis could be marginalized has also to be understood and contextualized within the thinking of a situation like that in America, where attacks on the scientific status of psychoanalysis and its results have enormously increased during the last decades—something that we are now starting to observe even in Europe and in England. The problem is, of course, whether the best way of defending psychoanalysis is to cut through its complexities and specific characteristics, even where problems related to its developmental issues are concerned, in the name of a linear and at times too simplistic notion of progress and the need to be "objective", being unable to withstand the enormous manipulative scientist power of the adversaries of psychoanalysis. Certainly we all know and have to realize the danger present in certain too bold "imaginative conjectures" concerning the inner life of the baby, in particular the tendency to transform what are inferences and hypotheses into dogmatic "actual facts" beyond discussion. Yet (to paraphrase the famous Hegelian dictum, "the Real is the Rational") is all that appears so "real" actually so "rational"?

It will, of course, be up to the reader to make up his or her own mind as far as the various viewpoints expressed in this book are concerned. There is no doubt, nevertheless, that although in the end the main speakers agreed to disagree on many issues, the possibility for the English-speaking audience of having a clearer idea of the reasons for their disagreement is an enrichment in itself, because it allows for a better understanding of the issues at stake.

Perhaps what was missing from this debate was a historical overview concerning the relationships between psychoanalysis and baby and child observations—the non-analytical ones and the psychoanalytically oriented ones too. In our field, indeed, they seem to have become very fashionable, particularly since the Second World War, both in England and in America. One has to say that the observations have become far more systematic and are carried out by an enormous number of people, in different countries, compared with what happened during the first decades of the history of psychoanalysis. But the relationship between psychoanalyst and baby observation has to be traced back to the origins of psychoanalysis itself, without forgetting that well before psychoanalysis ever existed there had been baby observations and quite a number of hypotheses even about the inner life of the baby and the child during the first, second, third year of its life! There had been even amazing awareness of the methodological issues concerned with observation itself—for example, the role played by the projections of the adult observer into the baby. Those projections were even considered gender-related—for instance, mothers were considered less able to observe than were fathers or male scientists in general (Steiner, in press)!

To understand the issues discussed by Green and Stern and others, it would perhaps have been very illuminating to see whether or how similar patterns of problems and even cultural differences in looking at those issues had existed before or during the first decades of the history of our discipline and how they were dealt with and, overall, whether there has been a line of continuity between the past and the present, or what has changed.[7]

[7] There is no doubt that extra-analytical observations (although questionable because of the way they were conducted, the kinds of babies or children who were observed, etc.) played a certain role in confirming and refining, at times, Freud's and the first child analysts' observations and hypotheses concerning the chronology of the development of the internal life of the baby and the child. It would be interesting, nevertheless, to compare contemporary research like that of Stern, for instance, with what baby observers had noticed in the past. Stern's (1985, 1995) views concerning the "emergent self" during the first two months of the life of the newborn baby, the "core self" starting with

Indeed, to mention *en passant* just a few examples, can references to "the infantile" in psychoanalysis, to the notion of primary narcissism in particular and its chronology in the life of the baby or to the existence or non-existence of early object relationships and to sexuality of the baby, can all this really be conceived without making *any link* to the background in which Freud and his first colleagues were educated and were working in Vienna, Budapest, Berlin, and London (Steiner, in press)? Can it be done without considering the impact of the work of Preyer (1882) and Baldwin (1895)? But most importantly, can it be done without forgetting the seminal paper by Darwin (1877) on the observation of his own infant, which had an enormous importance for the development of baby observation both outside and inside psychoanalysis (Conrad, 1998)? It is also difficult to imagine certain of Freud's hypotheses regarding the baby without referring, although with caution, to the researches of a neurologist like Flechsig concerning the myelinization of the nervous apparatus in the newborn baby. With the exception of Darwin's paper, which nevertheless was constantly quoted by Preyer, Baldwin, and others, Freud knew all those works perfectly well. Of course, he made up his own mind about all this, but there is no doubt that he took these works into consideration. Some echoes of these complex interactions between the newborn psychoanalysis and its extra-analytical background are present in the quotation with which I opened this Introduction. But besides Freud and what one could find about his own (although scanty) baby observations in the "Minutes of the Vienna Psychoanalytic Society", let alone, of course, his more famous clinical inferences (e.g. 1905d; 1909b; 1918b [1914], p. 13; 1919e, p. 177; 1920g, pp. 14–17), just think of Hug-Hellmuth's pioneering book of 1913 or of Bernfeld's seminal book of 1925 which deeply influenced Klein, too, as far as the problems of the earliest object

---

the second and third month, and the "subjective self" which can be observed between the seventh and the ninth month of the life of the baby still follow *grosso modo* the chronology and often develop and deepen observations and hypotheses that could be founded in many of the studies and observations of the major but even the lesser-known baby observers of the first decades of the twentieth century, if not before, both in Europe and in America. Of course, the observations became more systematic and precise with the passing of time (Steiner, in press).

relations of the baby, the importance of the weaning phase, and the chronology of the depressive position were concerned. Those analysts tried to use baby observation not just to confirm Freud's views but also to refine them, relying at times on an extremely rich although rather chaotic wealth of observations coming from extra-analytical sources. Or just think of the complex relationship between some of Anna Freud's most-gifted young colleagues—Hartmann, Spitz, Eckstein, Hellmann, Frankl, and others—and the research on baby and child observation by the Bühlers in Vienna during the 1930s. Even Esther Bick was influenced by the Bühlers (Steiner, in press), not to mention Susan Isaacs, who also studied the Bühlers and discussed Piaget in particular and was working at that time under Klein's influence in London. They all used observations to confirm support for their psychoanalytic persuasions or to counteract criticisms of their own views.

But to give another example: could Lacan's "mirror stage" (1977, pp. 1–7) really be conceived without *any* reference to the work of J. Baldwin (1895), Charlotte Bühler (1928), and even Henri Wallon (1949), as Lacan himself, although reluctantly, acknowledges (Macey, 1988; Roudinesco, 1993). Baldwin, Bühler, and Wallon, incidentally, made their observations following what Preyer and even Darwin had already noticed concerning the role played in the baby's development by the fact that at around the fourth or fifth month of its life it seems to start recognizing itself in the mirror . Or can one really claim that Winnicott's "transitional object" could have been conceived without any link to the observations made by him for years as a paediatrician? Winnicott even acknowledged the importance of Merell Middlemore's researches on what she called "the nursing couple" (1942) in persuading him that there was no such thing as a mother separated from the baby (see King & Steiner, 1992, p. 820). And Middlemore's researches, although analytically oriented and influenced by Klein to a certain point, were based on her wealth of observations as an obstetrician. Winnicott himself acknowledged the usefulness of baby observation for psychoanalysis, to a certain point, to prove but also to discard what he considered were too speculative hypotheses concerning the development of the baby, provided that baby observation is not used in a crude way and does not aim at constructing a psychology of early infancy, relying only on itself, because it is unable to do that (Winnicott, 1957, pp. 112–114). Probably my reading of Winnicott differs slightly here from certain of Green's statements.

But there is no doubt that, as psychoanalysts, we should not forget the specificity of psychoanalysis and the unique value of its interpretative instrument, as Green emphasizes. Perhaps in this context it would be useful to quote directly what Klein (1944, pp. 773–775) observed during the Freud–Klein Controversial Discussions. Here, the issue of how much weight to give to extra-analytical observations was discussed at length, and evaluating the objectivity of those baby observations was of paramount importance for the Freudians in their criticisms of Klein. But the reverse was also true, because Klein and her colleagues also used them to confirm her hypotheses. At one point, Klein, referring herself to the seminal work of Bernfeld (1925) and his views about the necessity of an "intimate knowledge of the child's reactions" to be able fully to evaluate, for instance, the observations concerning the observable behaviour of the baby to the trauma of weaning, stated:

> The conclusion that even if facts were not "scattered" and acquired with "insufficient exactitude" as they are [Klein was referring to Bernfeld's expressions, putting them into quotation marks] we could not expect observation alone to get full proofs for the unconscious processes at work in infants seems a truism, but one which is worthwhile remembering, since the demand by a few contributors in these discussions for "direct" proofs seems to ignore this fact. [Klein, 1944, p. 775]

And Klein was referring to the analysis of small children that was done, of course, by an adult and therefore with all the problems related to her own hypothetical inferences, as she called them, to get the "intimate knowledge of the child's mind and particularly of his phantasy life" (p. 775).

What seemed to emerge with some evidential certainty from the historical study of the relationship between baby observation and psychoanalysis and the way psychoanalysts also used extra-analytical observations is the way in which over time various analysts have tried to *elasticize* Freud's notion of *Nachträglichkeit* with data coming from both baby observations and child analysis. (I have borrowed the expression "to elasticize" from Joseph

Sandler, 1983.) Of particular interest in this complex history, which could perhaps help the reader better to understand many of the different viewpoints of this book, are the Freud–Klein Controversial Discussions of the 1940s, as I have already mentioned. Indeed, in this case it is possible to see the attempt to justify the validity of certain hypotheses concerning the early intrapsychic life of the baby, using, for instance, in the case of Klein and her colleagues, child analysis, supported by baby observation but also by strong references both to the notion of "regression" and to a concept like "genetic continuity" advocated by Susan Isaacs (1943, p. 285), by Paula Heimann, who gave a very clear description of it (1944, p. 734), and even by Marjorie Brierley, who defined it as "our old friend the law of psychological determinism in modern dress" (see King & Steiner, 1992, p. 331).[8] At the same time, neither Klein, nor Isaacs, nor Heimann denied Freud's notion of *Nachträglichkeit*, to which, of course, Anna Freud and her co-workers were adamantly loyal. They used baby observations or data coming from neurology, biology, and physiology to criticize Klein's and her followers views, as in the case of Kate Friedlander (see King & Steiner, 1992, p. 407).

The importance given to the concept of "genetic continuity", linked to Klein's views on early splitting and primary unconscious phantasies, led to a particular interpretation of Freud's *Nachträglichkeit*. According to this interpretation, the earliest experiences

[8] Of course, one could claim that even Anna Freud and her co-workers believed in "genetic continuity", but they insisted more on regression. The problem is nevertheless the emphasis that was given to this principle to try to justify or disclaim the presence of, for instance, "primary unconscious phantasies" in the baby. Isaacs defines "genetic continuity" as follows: "Whether in posture, locomotor and manipulative skills, in perception, language, or early logic, any given phase can be shown to have developed out of preceding phases in an ascertainable and intelligible way alike, in general outline and specific detail" (Isaacs, 1943, p. 285). But see also Heimann's comments on Isaacs' statements: "In human development no mental abilities or function appear suddenly. Each has a history and each has its roots in the earliest phases. We are not yet able to trace out all the detailed steps of development in each function, but every increase in our detailed knowledge emphasizes the fact that there is continuity and that every function has its rudimentary form from the beginning of extrauterine life" (Heimann, 1944, p. 734).

were thought by the Kleinians to be more available in the analysis both of small children and of adults. And they are still thought to be so today. This legitimated even more, therefore, hypotheses concerning the earliest intrapsychic life of the baby. Baby observation done with an "analytic eye" (Heimann, 1944, p. 689) and based on those assumptions was used to corroborate and refine what was extrapolated from the analysis of small children and adults.

There is no doubt that in the case of Klein, and even of those British colleagues who were critically appreciative of her viewpoints, this allowed for a greater permeability or porosity (Steiner, 1998) between what—to use the Sandlers' model (1984, 1987)—one could today call "the present and the past unconscious", to which both Green and Stern refer in their papers (although with different degrees of agreement with it). This can be observed even in Segal's (1999) comments on the latest reformulations done by Joseph Sandler (1998) of his and Anne-Marie Sandler's ideas.

There could have been a certain usefulness in recalling all this and showing the way in which child analysis, baby observation done with an "analytic eye", and the use of the notion of genetic continuity constitute a specific way of looking at these problems in some areas of British research even today. Or maybe it would simply have complicated the issue! Nevertheless, Joseph Sandler, in a personal communication in September 1998, told me that the latest reformulations of his ideas included an attempt to reply in his own way to the way in which baby observation is used by the followers of Melanie Klein today. Just think of his notion of "templates" and so forth.[9] However, to explore those issues further would cause us to stray too far.

To allow the reader to become more acquainted with some of the more general epistemological issues present in the papers both of Green and Stern and of other participants at the meeting, Sandler thought that it would be appropriate to include in this book the exchange of views between André Green and Robert Wallerstein, one of the pioneers in empirical research in psychoanalysis in America. They discussed the relevance of empirical

[9] For this notion, see also A. M. Cooper, "Infant Research and Adult Psychoanalysis" (1989, p. 84).

research for psychoanalysis in the *I.P.A. Newsletter* of 1997. Well, perhaps even in this case it is worth while to remind the reader of some of Freud's statements on the same matter, not to claim that he was absolutely right and that we have to follow him dogmatically, but just to show how complicated the issues were already at the time and how aware he was of them. There is, of course, the letter he wrote to Saul Rosenzweig on 28 February 1934 (see Gay, 1988, p. 523), after Rosenzweig had presented Freud with some experimental studies designed to test the validity of several psychoanalytic propositions.

"While he found such investigations interesting", writes Peter Gay in his Freud biography (1988, p. 523), Freud saw little value in it "because", Freud claimed, "the wealth of dependable observations on which psychoanalytic investigations rests, makes them independent of experimental verification". But then Freud added: "Still it can do no harm."

But I also have in mind what Freud told Marie Bonaparte and Ernest Jones, quoted in his biography of Freud (Jones, 1957, Vol. II):

> Mediocre spirits demand of science a kind of certainty which it cannot give, a sort of religious satisfaction. Only the real, rare, true scientific minds can endure doubts which are attached to all our knowledge. I always envy the physicists and mathematicians who can stand on firm grounds. I hover, so to speak, in thin air. Mental events seem to be immeasurable and probably always will be so. [p. 418]

Obviously, one needs to contextualize Freud's observations historically, and one also has to say that perhaps his optimism concerning the firm grounds of the methodology of physics and mathematics, thinking of their developments in certain areas, was a bit exaggerated. And one could ask oneself, of course, whether his cautiousness concerning the measurability of mental events was due to lack of sophistication of the research of that time. But, of course, this is an open problem, one that nevertheless has enormous implications for the future.

Indeed, in the new millennium that is opening up in front of us, bearing in mind also what Green, Stern, Wallerstein, Sandler, and many other contributors to this book are claiming and the difficult situation and problems of contemporary psychoanalysis, there is no doubt that some of the most important critical debates to decide what we will have to consider as psychoanalysis or how to be a psychoanalyst or whether psychoanalysis will survive at all will develop around the nature of those "mental events" mentioned by Freud and whether or what can be "measured of them" or whether we have to accept, due to the nature of the unconscious and its way of working, that they will remain "probably . . . always . . . immeasurable".

PART I

CHAPTER ONE

What kind of research for psychoanalysis?

André Green

The noble term "research" carries such an amount of prestige that it is to be expected that any reference to it might compel one to bow before it. Unfortunately, compared with the richness of the clinical experience of psychoanalysis, the findings of researchers look very meagre. Therefore, one has to be very cautious about the pretence to leadership of those who stand behind research. As some of the results of the requirements to make research possible end with an oversimplification of psychoanalytic knowledge, defended as a precondition of the path that would lead psychoanalysis to a science of proven facts, it is essential to preserve what is specific to the psychoanalytic endeavour. This last task is not at all a simple one, as what appears evident is difficult to spell out. Hence the necessity of scrutinizing what is the real situation and the status of the relationship between practice and theory. The condition created by the dispersed understanding of both of these in today's psychoanalysis, all over the world, increases the difficulty of reaching a wide agreement.

Reproduced by permission from *International Psychoanalysis: The Newsletter of the International Psychoanalytical Association*, 5 (1996): 10–14.

For several years now, research in psychoanalysis has formed part of the programme of scientific meetings. At first sight, it seems unquestionable that psychoanalysis can benefit from research, as can any other discipline whose aim is to increase our knowledge. Nevertheless, I am convinced that unless one discusses precisely the contents of the concept, a great confusion can arise from the findings and discoveries that are labelled "research".

A very brief retrospective view cannot be avoided here. For Freud it was self-evident that psychoanalysis was a branch of science. He expressed himself unambiguously in the last of his *New Introductory Lectures*: "The Question of a *Weltanschaüung*" (1933a). He writes: "Our best hope for the future is that intellect—the scientific spirit, reason—may in process of time establish a dictatorship in the mental life of man" (p. 171). Nevertheless, his radical ideas on truth and his total confidence in scientific investigation were not always respectful of the criteria of science. In many circumstances, as we know, Freud overtly contradicted the scientific views of his time—for instance, in his ideas about phylogenetic traces—arguing that the future would prove that he was right. And from time to time, he would say that he was above all—which means even above his claim to be a scientist—a psychoanalyst.

So the question of the scientificity of psychoanalysis is not at all a clear issue. The psychoanalytic community is not unanimous. Many psychoanalysts, mainly in the United States, strongly adhere to the idea that psychoanalysis is a science. But we know that others prefer the idea that psychoanalysis belongs to hermeneutics. Riccardo Steiner (1995) has dealt with this topic recently. A third party will refute both issues; for these psychoanalysts, psychoanalysis belongs neither to science nor to hermeneutics. I have defended previously the idea that the ideal of psychoanalysis was to be part of science, but that the specificities of its practice and of its mode of thinking were not compatible with the ordinary requirements of scientific evidence. Moreover, I observed that the more the object of science dealt with the inanimate world, the more precise the scientific knowledge. When we get closer to the living substance, the questions become much more obscure and the enigmas more numerous. And when finally we reach the domain of psychic activity, the problems are extremely intricate and the ability to reach definite conclusions becomes very limited.

A new field in epistemology has recently been opened up, with such concepts as self-organization and hypercomplexity. Space limitations do not allow me to explain their differences from traditional thinking. In a few words, for hypercomplexity (see, for example, Atlan, 1994; Morin, 1991; Von Foerster, 1984) the crucial issues have to accept a certain degree of indeterminacy and to admit the undecidable. It becomes impossible to proceed to a closure of the problem, and we are compelled to agree on the openness of the questioning. If there is a domain in which these ideas seem to be relevant, psychic activity is surely the one. The biological and anthropological determinants of what we call "psychic" are heavy enough to be considered, though psychic activity appears as an original creation which emerges from their interaction, bringing to light its specific organization (or self-organization). The hypercomplex nature, not only of the brain but of the psyche, which has also to consider the role of groups, societies, and civilizations in their structural and historical perspectives, is the challenge of our century.

Are we so far from psychoanalysis? I do not believe so, because it is a methodological problem. We have to ask ourselves what method is appropriate for dealing with the type of material met with in our psychoanalytic experience. I came to the conclusion that as far as psychic activity was concerned (different in essence from neurological mechanisms and, needless to say, computers), science has had to change its parameters to do justice to the facts that it investigates. Even within its rigorously defined field, debates between philosophers of science hardly come to a conclusion (Chalmers, 1976; Dupuy, 1994; Green, 1991).

It is understandable that when we come to psychoanalysis and research, the first question concerns what we are trying to find. It is my belief that all the researches on the psychoanalytic cure have failed to discover truly significant facts. Recent examples seem to confirm my view (Vaughan & Roose, 1995). Moreover, disagreements on basic definitions question even the possibility of valid research that could shed some light on psychoanalytic facts observed in different parts of the world. For instance, is the definition of what is a psychoanalytic process the same in North America (and in different areas of that vast continent), South America (composed of diverse psychoanalytic traditions), and Europe (with an even larger diversity)? Up till now, the great contributors to psychoanalytic theory (Freud, Abraham, Ferenczi, Rank, Melanie Klein, Bion, Winnicott, Lacan, Hartmann, etc.) have all enriched our knowledge with their work stemming from their single mind and from the working through of their own experience with their patients. On the other hand, there is no one single major discovery for psychoanalysis which has emerged from research. Margaret Mahler, during a private exchange with me, has confessed that she had to recognize that, as far as the intrapsychic world was concerned, her research could not be of any use. If we think of more recent contributions—for instance, those of Daniel Stern (1985)—which in many points disagree with Margaret Mahler's (Mahler, Pine, & Bergman, 1975) findings, we can see that his research can be of interest for psychological knowledge but is of little help for psychoanalytic theory. This does not prevent Stern from strongly recommending psychoanalysts to give up some major concepts of theory. For instance, he concludes the non-existence of the stimulus barrier or even orality. It is obvious that a new ideology is at work. Fonagy (1998) tries to apply the discoveries of cognitive sciences to child psychoanalysis, but I still do not see how these apply to the psychoanalytic material he exposes. There is a neglect in most of the investigations of the specificity of what is intrapsychic and unconscious, and an underestimation of the parameters of the analytic situation related to the concept of the setting, with the implicit idea that an observational procedure of interpersonal relationships can better account for the object of psychoanalysis than the speculation of psychoanalysts drawn from their therapeutic experience. We can also observe that Freud's initial definitions of psychoanalysis have now undergone substantial changes with the claim that psychoanalysis is a "theory of personality", a definition that fits better with a psychological perspective than with a psychoanalytical one.

Here is a major issue. It is not at all agreed universally that psychoanalysis can be equated with psychoanalytic psychology, whether this alludes to ego psychology or any other kind of psychology (e.g. self-psychology). Space limitations again do not allow me to develop this fundamental point of debate. In a few words, which I am sure will raise a lot of disagreement, the ego of the second topographical model of Freud has been interpreted in a distorted way. First, the differences between the ego of pre-psychoanalytic psychology and the Freudian concepts of the ego lessened. Second, taking the ego as the central point for the interpretation of what went on during analytic treatment was misleading, as the id, being considered out of reach, was more and more undervalued. Consequently, the entire theory of the drives was progressively rejected in favour of a psychological interpretation of "behaviour". Third, getting rid of the drives was an important move towards a psychologically centred theory. The challenge of the theory of object relations, which in the beginning enriched psychoanalytic theory, superseded the theory of drives and led to an oversimplification, which reduced the understanding of psychoanalytic processes in terms of interpersonal relationships. Harry Stack Sullivan (1953) was back! It is urgent to proceed to a revision of theory, based on the necessity to articulate the intrapsychic and the intersubjective points of view in a psychoanalytical (and not psychological) frame of mind. What difference between psychological and psychoanalytical? I will answer concisely, because of space limitations, that psychology is bound to restrict its domain to consciousness (at its extreme it can reach the preconscious, but not beyond that point), whereas psychoanalytic metapsychology deals with what is beyond the wall of consciousness and has its roots in the body. Desire is not equal to motivation or intentionality.

What about other attempts, such as the important investigations of Robert S. Wallerstein (1986)? These works, which are centred on psychoanalytic experience, represent tremendous efforts to try to systematize the diversities of therapeutic knowledge. But here again, we come to psychoanalytic aporias—for instance, the debates about the reference to observational data, clinical facts, and theoretical concepts. At first sight, it could be self-evident that our concepts should be derived from observational data only. But a deeper reflection shows this to be an oversimplification. It is clear, for instance, thinking of Freud's findings and theory, that many essential concepts such as the unconscious or transference could not be observed directly but had to be deduced, as he himself stated. So deduction cannot be avoided in the debate about psychoanalytic conclusions. Recently, a vast inquiry on clinical facts and their conceptualization in psychoanalysis has offered us the opportunity to become aware of the absence of agreement on some basic notions on which the major part of our work stands. It is impossible to underestimate the importance of our divergences on these foundations of psychoanalytic thinking.

Am I rejecting the possibility of research in psychoanalysis? Even if I have a strong feeling about the necessity of putting under close scrutiny such an obvious and common-sense idea of the utility of research, I would like rather to emphasize what limitations occur from the very narrow basis on which it is based in our discipline. There are entire fields of knowledge highly valued by Freud—such as the history of civilization, religions, art, and institutions—that can teach us a great deal about the nature and function of the unconscious: dimensions that are not part of our present research. The objection that it is difficult to include these disciplines in the projects of research is less important than the fact that these references are completely absent from the minds of the researchers. I do not question the necessity for studies based on a significant number of patients to compare what can be observed from the range of confrontations with experience. But we must also know that the facts that lend themselves to this type of investigation are of limited significance. I also accept the idea that it is interesting to observe more carefully the development of the infant, but psychological development should not be confused with the psychoanalytic one and I have doubts about the possibility of describing this last through procedures of observation. I must add that the claim of some researchers of having been psychoanalytically trained does not constitute for me a sufficient guarantee of the validity for psychoanalysis of their findings. Screen memories are a psychoanalytic notion. We could also speak of "screen trainings".

Having given a lot of thought to the present crisis of psychoanalysis as it manifests itself in International Psychoanalytic Association (IPA) congresses, I came to the conclusion that the greater risk for the future of psychoanalysis is the decline and possible fall of the spirit of psychoanalysis, the specific mental state that inhabits the psychoanalyst during his or her work and thinking. Our task is to keep alive that spirit. I am not at all sure that this moral task can be better ensured by what is today called research in psychoanalysis. I strongly wish to be proved wrong.

CHAPTER TWO

Psychoanalytic research: where do we disagree?

Robert S. Wallerstein

I invited André Green to provide his brief, but densely packed, evaluation of the psychoanalytic research enterprise as it is currently represented within psychoanalytic ranks, in the expectation—which has been richly rewarded—that he would present persuasively the cogent and proper questions that any effort to apply the canons of empirical science to the highly subjectivistic and unconsciously rooted phenomena of the psychoanalytic situation would inevitably raise in the psychoanalyst imbued with what Green calls "the spirit of psychoanalysis, the specific mental state that inhabits the psychoanalyst during his or her work and thinking" (p. 26). Without trying to define this elusive but vital "spirit", I think we can all—the avowed psychoanalytic researchers included—resonate to this *cri de coeur* to preserve intact the fundamental essence of what Freud innovated and bequeathed to us as the most revealing way of comprehending the normal and abnormal workings of the human mind.

Reproduced by permission from *International Psychoanalysis: The Newsletter of the International Psychoanalytical Association*, 5 (1996): 15–17.

Given this fundamental agreement on the vantage point from which psychoanalytic research, or any other purportedly psychoanalytic activity, should be viewed, where do Green and I possibly differ in the conclusions that we draw when we consider the present state and the unfolding future prospects of that research enterprise? Green's brief essay is clearly packed with an intricate array of interrelated conceptions, some stated directly, and even starkly, without the space for the elaboration that he could so richly provide, and some indicated only by passing allusion. A proper assessment and response would indeed also require the elaboration that the limitations of space do not allow. I will single out only two organizing and overriding themes in Green's statement to which I will react in an equally didactically, expository, and telescoped way. The first theme is that of the conceptual (and methodological) difficulties of trying to do properly scientific psychoanalytic research in full harmony with the vital "spirit" of psychoanalysis—that is, research that is simultaneously faithful both to the highly subjectivistic and complex data of the psychoanalytic consulting-room and to the so-called objective canons of the empirical scientific inquiry. That should be, after all, the heart of what we call psychoanalytic research. The second theme advanced by Green that I wish to respond to is the distinction that he draws between psychoanalysis focused on the unconscious realm of desire in all its myriad representations, and psychology as a science of human development and behaviour derived from observable and consciously available data.

On the first of these major themes, that of the difficulty and complexity of proper psychoanalytic research, I feel in fundamental agreement with Green's position, if I read him properly. For if, as Freud claimed, psychoanalysis belongs properly to the sciences and not to the humanities—that is, if there is to be progressive advance of knowledge, building incrementally on prior observation and conceptualization—then scientific research, in the sense of devising methods to test whether formulations about observed or inferred phenomena are more plausible and more in accord with observation than alternative formulations, is of the essence of that incremental knowledge advance. To do this can be dauntingly difficult and complicated just because, as Green correctly points out, the data we deal with are not of the mechanisms of the inanimate world of nature (the natural sciences) or of the operative mechanisms of the living world of flora and fauna where the phenomena of mind are not under study (the biological sciences), but are the quintessentially mental concerns of desire and will and intention in all their subjectivity and elusiveness and ambiguity that are, indeed, the essence of psychoanalysis. Yet science is not defined by its content, but by its method of inquiry, and the challenge for psychoanalytic research is to accomplish its necessary work by methods devised in such a way as not to do violence to the nature, or "spirit", of the enterprise being studied. This—those of us formally committed to the necessities and possibilities of proper psychoanalytic research feel—should be doable, albeit with real difficulty, and in this I think that, in theory at least, Green agrees.

Green does complain rightly that up to this point not a great deal in the way of psychoanalytic advance—in the sense of "major discovery"—has yet emerged from formal psychoanalytic research, and with this I ruefully agree, though much hinges on definitional matters, what we mean by "major discovery" and by "scientific advance". He also alludes to the fact that some of what has been offered as psychoanalytic research has been by methods, borrowed too unthinkingly from other realms of research, that have reduced or glossed over the "degree of indeterminacy" and the "hypercomplexity" inherent in the data of psychoanalysis (its "clinical facts") and thus has obscured and trivialized, rather than clarified, psychoanalytic knowledge—and unhappily that is all too true. But he also refers to what he calls the "important investigations" of the Psychotherapy Research Project of the Menninger Foundation (Wallerstein, 1986) which was an effort at least to, in Green's terms, "systematize the diversities of therapeutic knowledge", or, in our terms, to go beyond the limitations of the familiar psychoanalytic single-case study, into formal and systematic research on the psychoanalytic process in a manner that we described as "at once meaningful and responsive to the subtlety and complexity of the phenomena and at the same time scientific in the best sense of that term (loyalty to the reality principle, as here embodied in appropriate canons of scientific inference)" (Wallerstein & Sampson, 1971, p. 11). I think that Green agrees in full with the spirit of the credo just stated and with the paths proposed in the article from which it is cited, to live up to it, though with his substantial reservations about the practicalities of the endeavour or of the real successes in the sense of empirical knowledge advances in psychoanalysis that will be achieved thereby. But that itself is an empirical question, and the proof of that pudding will be in the eating.

Now, even more briefly, for Green's second theme—that of the relationship between psychoanalysis and psychology as sciences. Here I feel that we have a real disagreement in viewpoint. Green asserts a fundamental distinction between the two. He states: "What difference between psychological and psychoanalytical? I will answer concisely . . . that psychology is bound to restrict its domain to consciousness (at its extreme, it can reach the preconscious but not beyond that point), whereas psychoanalytic metapsychology deals with what is beyond that wall of consciousness and has its roots in the body. Desire is not equal to motivation or intentionality" (p. 25). Here we clearly do differ, but the difference to me, to a significant extent, is a definitional difference and this hinges, to me, on how it is heuristically most useful to try to define both psychology and psychoanalysis. Here I start with Freud: "Psycho-analysis is a part of psychology; not of medical psychology in the old sense, not of the psychology of morbid processes, but simply of psychology. It is certainly not the whole of psychology, but its substructure and perhaps even its entire foundation" (Freud, 1926e, p. 252). That is what Green calls psychology (limited to the understanding of conscious mental processes) and what Freud therefore named "depth psychology". I would prefer to encompass all as psychology, ranging, within one unifying framework, from the manifest surfaces to the unknown depths of the human mind. The advantage of amalgamating rather than separating the two is that, to me, this is a more heuristically useful rendering of the phenomena of the mind, in all their intermingled and fluid continuity, from external to internal, from material reality to psychic reality, from clinical fact to governing fantasy, and from objectively conscious to subjectively unconscious. To separate these into separate realms of inquiry would be, to me, both artificial and unnatural; to assign conscious and unconscious mental phenomena to differing realms of inquiry would, in my mind, do violence to their inherent interpenetrations and hamper our collective search for that most comprehensive understanding of the mind in action that psychoanalytic psychology promises us.

I wish that there were more time and space here both for André Green and for myself. But perhaps we have between us in this interchange clarified somewhat what the issues are in our varying perspectives upon the psychoanalytic research enterprise in a way that is useful to others and will in turn elicit a wider array of responses from others equally concerned with the nature of psychoanalysis and how best to enlarge the understandings that it offers us.

CHAPTER THREE

Response to Robert S. Wallerstein

André Green

In accepting Robert S. Wallerstein's invitation, I knew that our mutual esteem and respect for each other, which characterize a long-standing friendship, would not prevent important disagreements. If there is a need for a debate, inevitably there are implicit or explicit opposing views. The condensed form of my statements, due to space limitations, has not allowed me sufficient clarification. My partner recognizes this fairly. His comment has the virtue of revealing where obscurities remain.

About the "spirit" of psychoanalysis: though I am sure that any full-time practising analyst understands what I am here alluding to, I will label it in an oblique way, speaking here of what constitutes the ground of psychoanalytic identity at work. There are sufficient signs among the ranks of psychoanalysts that this identity is presently less assured with the evolution of our discipline. Sometimes, there is a feeling that it is threatened with fading away, if not disappearing under different influences. Some of these belong to factors outside psychoanalysis, and some others within.

Reproduced by permission from *International Psychoanalysis: The Newsletter of the International Psychoanalytical Association*, 5 (1996): 18–21.

My emphasis on the state of mind operating in the analytic session is not precise enough, as here, too, misunderstanding may arise. (Green, 1993a). In the context of the present discussion, to speak of the highly subjectivist approach of the analyst is not only meant to oppose it to the objectivistic methods that are required in research, but to underline the peculiar if not unique functioning of the psychoanalytic subject in the listening process, in the setting. What I am alluding to is the oscillating and alternating provisional constructions that take place, sometimes simultaneously and sometimes in a sequential way, during psychic work. Psychic work has to be related here to analogous processes well known in psychoanalytic theory, such as the dream work, the work of mourning, and so forth.

Let us give a simplified description in which we will designate the sequence of free associated thoughts in the session, which we will arbitrarily name according to the succession of letters in the alphabet. These are elements in the chain constituted by the material designed in a series *a, b, c, d,* . . . . The question is how the series will acquire a meaning even in the apparent incoherence, due to free association, in the manifest content, which will lead to radical transformation of the latent content, appearing in opposite relationship to the manifest. Let us take, for instance, element *c*, which arouses some attention in the analyst's mind. Such an element is associated with the manifest meaning following the sequence preceding it with *a* and *b*. But after a while, some other further element, let us say *m* or *n*, enlightens its relationship to *c* and makes it appear in a new light quite different from its original meaning. Then, some other relationship linking the new relationship between *m, n,* and *c* is grounded by a relationship that has escaped the analyst's attention with some intermediary links with, let us suppose, *g* and *h*. This entirely new set of connections gives birth to the repressed and the unconscious, with the new dimension, which has to be accounted for, that the resistances and mechanisms of defence are also unconscious. We see that all these processes, which happened in the silence of the analyst, appear sometimes, all of a sudden, in a glance that gives meaning retrospectively to *c* and to its inclusion in the chain of words and representations in a view that contradicts the previous manifest meaning it had when it was first heard. We see here that reversal of meaning, which is coexistent with the intervention of the defences, mainly repression, totally escapes the possibility of being observed in any way other than the type of awareness stemming from the clinical situation. If we add to that that our abstract representation, in terms of *a, b, c, d, . . .*, in order to give a clearer image of what we are talking about, relates in fact to different types of psychic activity all intermingled in the associative network—that is, words, thing presentations, affects, potential actions, drive representatives, and so on—we can realize what we mean by hypercomplexity. It is doubtful to think of findings (which are by necessity all reduced to a single scale of expressions: verbal or perceptual) where this specific complexity related to the psychic apparatus will ever be reached, not even mentioning how it is even more increased going through the filter of transference and countertransference exchanges or through the relationships of the present and the past. What I am stating here is that psychic processes cannot be observed, as their outcome in one channel does not do justice to their nature and structure, and, also, that the accounts of psychoanalytic or psychotherapeutic cures grouped in connections (Wallerstein, 1986) can only more or less give very limited information on the specific mechanism, of which only psychoanalytic theory can enlighten.

On child observation: I repeat that I think that the problem of child observation cannot be dissociated from the theoretical framework in which the findings are formalized. Let us take a very simple example: the transitional object in Winnicott's (1953) work. Considered as a fact, the transitional object is a very ordinary feature known long ago to any mother. If we compare the transitional object with the theory of transitional phenomena and transitional space, the gap between the fact and the theory leads to two remarks: first, it is impossible to deduce from the facts observed the lowest level of the theoretical conclusions drawn by Winnicott; and, second, the gap between the transitional object and the idea of a transitional space is even more impossible to imagine in the perspective of so-called research.

Let us now shift to another example. The understanding of psychosis from the psychoanalytic point of view is a task full of questions and obscurities. The concept proposed by Bion (1962) of the container and the contained which is entirely drawn from experience has proven very useful to those working in that field. No other research was here set up except that which took place in the mind of the analyst in his consulting-room.

Let us examine other findings that have been discovered through systematic research—for instance, separation anxiety in the work of Margaret Mahler (Mahler et al., 1975). Its germ can be traced to Freud in *Inhibitions, Symptoms and Anxiety* (1926d [1925]), but it is only within the setting up of research that it was brought out and has been adopted largely among many psychoanalysts, if not all. Nevertheless, it appears to me that unfortunately what has been described under that label has led to constantly growing misinterpretations. It finally became a behavioural notion, its effect being taken on the level of external evidence of its manifestations (see the work of Bowlby, 1969, 1973, 1980, among others) more than driving us to a deeper interpretation of what went on intrapsychically. For instance, what were the consequences for the psychic organization, its influence on symbolization, or the effects of the alternation between presence and absence in the mind? Such questions, unfortunately, were not raised. Moreover, what we have witnessed has been the challenge of Mahler's work scrutinized through advances in research claiming for more "scientificity". Such an approach can be found in the work of Daniel Stern questioning Mahler's conceptions and offering alternative views, which I will not discuss for the time being, limiting myself to observing that, with Stern's conceptions, we are even more and more removed from psychoanalytic theory. Obviously, the aim is to substitute the extant psychoanalytic theory with a new one that is supposed to be better, completely "cleaned" of ideas not consistent with the procedures of so-called research, as if it were assumed that we could translate into procedures of research everything that is experienced in the clinical situation.

This, of course, is not the type of research in which Wallerstein is involved, but one cannot deny that it is the mainstream in what is practised under that name. Anyhow, I have doubts about the goals or the prospects of future psychotherapy research: "the true comparative study of methods and results across theoretical frameworks and across 'schools', using the kinds of mutually agreed-upon definitions, instruments, methods and criteria which will make such comparisons meaningful" (Wallerstein, 1986, p. 745).

Psychoanalytic identity: I come now to our major point of disagreement, on the difference between psychological and psychoanalytical. Wallerstein calls on Freud to support the idea of absence of difference between psychology and psychoanalysis. First, what Freud meant by psychology is very different from what was considered psychology in his time (which was in an embryonic state) and I am sure even more from what is considered psychology today. He considered psychology a "natural science". For instance, this naturalistic reference was consistent in Freud's mind with his conception of the drives as the base of the psychic apparatus, a hypothesis that is very largely rejected, especially among those who refer to the psychological conception of psychoanalysis. "Psychological psychology" (as opposed to psychology as a "natural" science) requires a reformulation of some of the most essential views of Freud. The gains of this revision are not unanimously agreed upon. Therefore, Wallerstein's disagreement with the idea of a distinction between the conscious and the unconscious, pleading for their coexistence within one unifying framework, seems to me impossible to sustain. Here Wallerstein will have to admit that he is totally contradicting Freud, who insisted on a clear distinction between the conscious/preconscious and the unconscious. In the above-cited example of the processes that take place in the analyst's mind, the role of the preconscious is essential as a mediator. The processes we shall deduce as supposedly belonging to the unconscious are of a totally different nature and involve a different logic to the conscious one, rejecting in my view any gradual approach from the conscious to the unconscious and implying some sort of mutative understanding. I see in Wallerstein's position the reflection of a point of view that we can see expressed in many current psychoanalytic papers of a totally integrative view encompassing all psychic features in an overall understanding, which to me contradicts the idea of the existence of an unconscious. This approach threatens to dissolve the specificity of psychoanalysis. The amalgamation—Wallerstein's expression—increases the risk of underestimating the load of the unconscious and the way it is so contrary to the linking mechanisms of secondary processes. I am not very hopeful of the building of a new psychoanalytic thought in a new kind of general psychology. If psychoanalysis wants to preserve what it has to say on the human mind that no other discipline is able to say, we have to watch the direction we take. It is here that we really have to consider the implication of Wallerstein's observation: "science is not defined by its content but by its methods of inquiry" (p. 29). We are still in want of the method for research that is coherent, not with the content of psychoanalysis, but with the type of thinking that is its true object. I regret to say that my feeling on the method adopted up till now has twisted the nature of the object. If the proof of the pudding is in the eating, an even stronger evidence is in its indigestibility.

PART II

CHAPTER FOUR

Science and science fiction in infant research

André Green

"Everything has been already said. Without any doubt.
If words haven't changed their meaning;
and meaning its words."

Jean Paulhan, from "Introduction aux Œuvres complètes"

Introductory remarks

In recent years I have had the opportunity to express a number of criticisms about what is called "research" in psychoanalysis. I suppose this was the reason for inviting me to participate in this meeting at University College. This is not the first time Daniel Stern and I meet as representatives of opposing points of view. We have had dialogues in Geneva, Naples, and Monaco. I ought to feel guilty about Daniel Stern because he happens to treat my work with greater benevolence than I treat his. In fact, I do not feel guilty because there is nothing personal in my opposition, and also because any careful reader will be able to see that if he quotes my work with appreciative comments—especially my paper "The

Dead Mother" (Green, 1986a)—he curbs my descriptions in order to make them fit his own point of view. Finally, he tries to show how his perspective includes mine—but the contrary is true. So even if I am grateful for his favourable comments, I remain, to my regret, in disagreement with him. Is that not why we are here today?

Earlier debates

When I asked Joseph Sandler and Peter Fonagy for some recent references on infant research, they sportingly communicated to me Peter H. Wolff's uncompromising paper, "The Irrelevance of Infant Observation for Psychoanalysis" (1996). It was fair to send me a work that was supportive of my point of view. This particular debate, which appeared in the *Journal of the American Psychoanalytic Association*, is of great importance. Anyone who is really concerned with the topic should read it, because in it the controversy is widened and raises general considerations much beyond the limits of infant research. The interest of Wolff's contribution is heightened by the qualifications of the author. He was a pioneer in the field of infant observation while he was still a candidate at the Boston Psychoanalytic Institute—but, as we shall see, psychoanalytic qualifications do not necessarily guarantee psychoanalytic validity. Of course, it is impossible to summarize here the debate to which seven colleagues contributed, and in any case summarizing would run the risk of discouraging you from reading it in full. I have to confess that I felt in agreement with only one discussant, Barnaby B. Barratt, who was totally unknown to me. Later I shall return to some of the points developed in that discussion, but for the moment I will only mention Peter Wolff's remark that "neither inferences about the observed infant's subjective experience nor eclectic research strategies that integrate empirical data and inferences about the infant's affective self will contribute significantly to psychoanalytic psychology as defined above; they are therefore essentially irrelevant for psychoanalysis as a psychology of idiosyncratic personal meanings and hidden motives" (p. 386). Wolff considers that the evidence from infant observations does not justify major revisions of psychoanalysis, and he says that "The psychological theories that emerge from such evidence differ so fundamentally from Freud's perspective on the human condition that their links to psychoanalysis appear irretrievably broken" (p. 386). And, finally, the relation to the psychoanalytic talking cure is no longer discernible. Some will probably think that Peter Wolff went too far. I think he did not go far enough, though his paper points in the right direction. I recall that my first objections appeared in my paper "L'enfant modèle" (1979), which had many arguments that were also present in Wolff's subsequent paper.

I regret that many of you have missed the possibility of becoming acquainted with these exchanges. Wolff's paper is not outside the scope of our meeting. He addresses the work of two authors, Daniel Stern and Robert Emde, with whom Peter Fonagy is a close collaborator. However, in my opinion, the whole debate turned into a dialogue of the deaf, and in order to avoid the repetition of such a situation I want to take some time to develop two preliminary points.

The spiritual families of psychoanalysis

First, it is obvious that the analytic community is split, and as a consequence the healing idea arose of searching for a common ground. By now this has led to somewhat artificial concordances, such as the meeting of the Kleinian concept of projective identification with intersubjectivity and enactment, used today by the "intersubjectivists" (see Gabbard, 1995). It is not enough to list the analysts according to their membership of various movements, for we have Ego Psychologists, Self Psychologists, Kleinians, Winnicottians, Lacanians, and others. However, it seems more accurate to say that quite apart from their belonging to one or other psychoanalytic sect, psychoanalysts are grouped in large "spiritual families" with kinship relationships which include siblings, cousins, distant relatives, and also outsiders. This does not, of course, favour the scientific validity of psychoanalytic theory. Olds and Cooper (1997) recently published a Guest Editorial in the *International Journal of Psycho-Analysis,* and I have to confess that, with all due respect to my eminent colleagues, it raised in me a feeling of how incredibly naive the authors are. Their exposition of the mind–brain problem calls for debate with regard to every sentence they wrote. This is not from the point of view of the "science of psychoanalysis", as such a science does not exist, but rather of psychoanalytic thinking. An editorial in the same journal was published by Robert Emde and Peter Fonagy (1997) with the suggestive title, "An Emerging Culture for Psychoanalytic Research". Emerging is not a banal adjective, for it refers to an important concept in the epistemology of biology. It is also used extensively by Daniel Stern and has a precise meaning in other theoretical contexts. It is clear from the enthusiastic tone of the Editorial that scientific research in psychoanalysis is now establishing itself as one of those spiritual families that I shall arbitrarily call the "objectivists". I consider them, in my personal classification, as foreigners, alien to me within our multicultural community. An important sum of money has been given by the International Psychoanalytical Association (IPA) to their Committee on Research, headed by Robert Wallerstein, chair of the advisory board of the IPA on research. Peter Fonagy chairs the Research Committee. As everyone knows, students go where the money is. So we have an urgent need to evaluate psychoanalytic research.

What are psychoanalytic writings about?

Why is the psychoanalytic tribe divided into clans? My answer is the following. Psychoanalysts, who create psychoanalytic literature, write less about their work than about what they think. Even in the case of so-called clinical papers, the most clinical of the contributions are presented through the understanding—that is, through the conceptual framework—of the psychoanalyst. We can recall David Tuckett's (1994a) concern when, as Editor of the *International Journal of Psycho-Analysis*, he asked: "What is a clinical fact?" The question is unavoidable, and relatively specific to psychoanalysis, because the majority of psychoanalysts do not seem to be informed of a concept presented by Jean-Luc Donnet and myself called "L'Écart théorico–pratique" [The Gap between Theory and Practice] (1973). Theory in psychoanalysis is by definition more distant from practice than one might wish for. This is a fact, a clinical and epistemological fact. In some cases, the gap can be intentionally increased for the purpose of advancing speculation, sometimes to a point at which many readers will abandon their assent to what is expounded. In other words, in any paper, the analyst's thinking always predominates over the facts. It is useless to discuss the content of a paper if one does not analyse the analyst's assumptions. This can give rise to paradoxical situations: if an analyst has skills in thinking and a very limited number of patients or candidates in supervision, he can nevertheless produce a very attractive theory. It would be hard to show that the theory, though appealing, is an abstraction, which can be fascinating but is unfortunately not linked to experience. At times it is easy to grasp what the analyst is thinking, and some writers state it explicitly. However, at other times it is not entirely clear what a writer thinks, either because he is unwilling to expose himself or because this aspect is not crystal-clear in his mind. Fortunately it is very helpful to consult the list of references cited in a paper. If we look at the contributors to the Peter Wolff debate, such an exploration is very rewarding. One knows better what authors have in mind by examining their references than by simply reading what they have written, without knowing what they themselves have read. Absent references are also significant.

I consulted the bibliography in a paper by Daniel Stern, "One Way to Build a Clinically Relevant Baby" (1994). If I omit the references to Stern's own work, there are 62 items, of which only 9 are related to psychoanalysis. A similar investigation of a paper by Emde, Kubicek, and Oppenheimer (1997a) shows 28 psychoanalytic works (the authors' excluded) out of a total of 94. Of course, there is nothing wrong in extending one's knowledge. The question is whether non-psychoanalytic works are simply supplements to our information or are opposed to it. For the most part, the non-psychoanalytic authors quoted are openly opposed to psychoanalysis. More specifically, their work reflects conceptions that deny what I dare to call the "psychoanalytic state of mind". If such opposition did not exist, there would be no reason for the fierce attacks against psychoanalysis we experience nowadays. One conclusion can be drawn: information from within and outside psychoanalysis is of no value if the basic assumptions of the authors are not scrutinized and critically assessed. Unfortunately, for much of the time, those psychoanalysts who support the so-called scientific trend do not demonstrate impressive qualities in that domain. All this reminds me of the French joke about "skylark pâté". Skylark pâté is a delicious food. Unfortunately, there are not enough skylarks available to supply all those people who want to eat some. So the cooks blend a mixture in order to be able to meet the demands of their customers. They dilute it with some other ingredient. Finally, the new pâté is composed of one skylark and one horse to make the mixture. The skylark here is the psychoanalytic literature, which is then mixed with the horse of all other disciplines. It can reasonably be expected that the resulting flavour will hardly evoke the taste of the poor psychoanalytic skylark. If one agrees that psychoanalysts write as much about what they think as about what they do, it may follow that what they do professionally outside the analytic setting will significantly affect what they think about when undertaking clinical psychoanalysis. Alternatively, what they think determines their choice of work outside the consulting-room. Note that I am not saying that a psychoanalyst should not do anything outside the consulting-room. I am only saying that the other activity may effectively impinge on one's thinking about psychoanalysis. Work outside the analytic setting, as we know, can take place in a very wide field; it includes working in institutions, sometimes with unanalysable patients, as well as teaching. With regard to the latter, what is taught is of some importance, whether it be psychiatry, psychology, physiology, literature, or history. Last, but not least, there is research.

On the relations between science and psychoanalysis

It should be strongly emphasized that, at present, science has a position that cannot be compared with anything else. Today, science is synonymous with truth—with or without Popper's (1959) criteria. If something is not validated by the scientific method, it is regarded as negligible. One worn-out argument put forward by the "scientific believers" is, if I may say so, that if one is not scientific then one has to be—whether one likes it or not—a hermeneuticist. This is a polite way of saying that one is of a religious mind, because this was the original field of hermeneutics; or one is told that one is a sceptic or has a relativistic mind. I am nothing of the kind, nor are some of the people who agree with my criticisms of psychoanalytic research. If by hermeneutics we want to qualify an epistemological attitude that gives interpretation a central place, then I accept that I am a "hermeneuticist". But as far as psychoanalysis is concerned, some of the members of my spiritual family (e.g., Riccardo Steiner, Jean Laplanche) object to being labelled as such.

It is easy to show that in the debate between science and psychoanalysis another conclusion has to be drawn: the scientific method till the present has proved to be sterile in psychoanalysis. As far as the philosophy of science is concerned, the results are rather disappointing. There are also spiritual families in philosophy, and the debate has to be opened more widely. Ricoeur (1977) is not a minor philosopher—he also defends himself against the charge of having tried to bring Freud's work into the field of hermeneutics.

The great mathematician and philosopher, René Thom, who was interested in the models of psychoanalysis, wrote in "La science malgré tout" (1968): *"Tout ce qui est rigoureux est insignifiant"* [Everything that is rigorous is insignificant]. René Thom is a recipient of the Fields Medal, equivalent to the Nobel Prize. G. Edelman, a Nobel prize winner, has written a book entitled *Bright Air, Brilliant Fire* (1992), which was dedicated to both Darwin and Freud. In it, Edelman presents a very severe critique of cognitive sciences, one usually ignored by the cognitivists. He attacks those who rely on "simple minded behaviourism", with their "extraordinary misconception of the nature of thought, reasoning [and] meaning" (p. 228). He says of the conceptions of cognitive science (alluding mainly to Jerry Fodor: see, for example, Fodor, 1981, 1992), "It is one of the most remarkable misunderstandings in the history of science" (p. 228). He adds a comment that no psychoanalyst would dare to write. He expresses the hope "that some day the more vocal practitioners of cognitive psychology, and the frequently smug empiricists of neuroscience will understand that they have unknowingly subjected themselves to an intellectual swindle" (p. 229). I expect that many will say that this criticism does not apply to them. I am not sure about that.

When psychoanalysts' writings reflect their thinking more than their work, the unnoticed gap between theory and practice becomes tragically deep; indeed, it may become bottomless if the analysts' minds are influenced by their concerns when they are doing scientific research. Wolff speaks of "psychoanalytically informed" researchers. One can say, *après coup*, that many of them had what I call a "screen training" in psychoanalysis, which allows them to safeguard themselves from the reproach that they ignore psychoanalysis. I have met many of them during meetings, and their manifest misunderstanding of what psychoanalysis is was astonishing. Being listed in the Membership Roster of the International Psychoanalytical Association is no longer enough.

Freud, psychic activity and psychology

Another point I want to make is the following. The starting point of our knowledge is Freud's work. The fact that Joseph Sandler and his colleagues felt that there was a need for a book entitled *Freud's Models of the Mind* (Sandler, Holder, Dare, & Dreher, 1997) is an indication that Freud's work has not yet been digested, especially in English-speaking countries. There should be no confusion about this. I am neither saying that Freud must be our present frame of reference nor that we have to go back to him. I am simply saying that, if we want to know exactly where we are, it is impossible to arrive at a clear view of our current situation if we do not understand the evolution of psychoanalytic theory. A skimming of the theory will not do. A detailed examination is needed because Freud himself sometimes obscures his own specificity. When Peter Wolff says that he will limit his discussion to "Freudian psychoanalysis", he is blamed by some for using too wide a definition, and by others for using far too narrow a one. Obviously to be a "Freudian" today is not at all unambiguous. When Wolff says that "psychoanalytic theories should concern themselves with the phenomena subsumed under the concepts of unconscious ideas, hidden motives and repression" (p. 370), the statement seems to me very valuable, though its formulation is awkward and debatable.

Since the early 1950s, the profile of psychoanalytic theory has been modified. Freud's original discovery was about the part of the mind that he first called the unconscious and then the id. Because he had to "locate" his findings in a wider context, he successively built up two conceptions of the psychic apparatus, which he called a "fiction". The misconception, to which Freud himself contributed, was to think that he had simply built a general model of the mind. In fact, he only did this from the starting point of his discovery—that is, the unconscious and its further replacement by the id—a concept that is almost unanimously rejected today—though not by me. All the elaboration of the theory of mind is meant to justify the everlasting influence of the id on the later, or more differentiated, structures of ego and superego, which were supposed to have overcome the power of the id. The misconception became obvious when Heinz Hartmann proposed that psychoanalytic theory become a "general psychology". The failure of Hartmann's project is now blatant, as Martin Bergmann (1993) has demonstrated. I would add that Hartmann's failure rested on the illusion that he could present a more reasonable—that is, scientific—psychoanalytic theory. In psychoanalytic meetings nowadays, we still hear analysts who are convinced that psychoanalysis is a theory about the "total personality". This inevitably leads to the dilution of the specificity of psychoanalysis in the so-called totality. In "Psycho-Analysis" (1926f [1925])—a very accessible paper, written for the *Encyclopaedia Britannica*, Freud says : "The therapeutic influence of psychoanalysis depends on the replacement of unconscious mental acts by conscious ones and is effective within the limits of that factor" (p. 265). This shows clearly the limited objectives of psychoanalysis and locates its core.

Most of the time the rejection of drive (or instinct) theory and—later on—of Freud's metapsychology has tended to favour the idea of psychoanalysis as a "psychology". I have always thought that "depth psychology" was an ambiguous expression. And then there was a shift to a two-body psychology—another misleading idea. It is obvious that psychoanalysis should not be solipsistic, as it sometimes seems to be in Freud's descriptions, but one should be aware that it is a two-body psychology about only one person and specifically about that person's singularity. The general theory is, to use Bion's terminology, a theory of the mind from the vertex of the unconscious. But from there on the so-called two-body psychology shifted to the relational point of view, and from there to the observational. The interpersonal, the intersubjective, or the interactive have progressively replaced the intrapsychic. As the model of representation was replaced by the model of behaviour—or, more precisely, by the duality of perception and action—the more the core of Freudian discovery lagged behind. Of course, I expect that my opponents will say that to focus on one point does not prevent one from being attentive to the other. That is what they say, but that is not what they do, think, or write about. And finally, what do we have? We have extreme subjectivism in the analytic session, and extreme objectivism at the opposite end of the spectrum (current psychoanalytic research). But this is only the appearance. As far as researchers are concerned, they display an enormous amount of subjectivity in their conclusions. But it is time now to come to infancy, as I am sure you have waited too long. These introductory remarks were, at least in my opinion, unavoidable.

The infantile child and the real child

In the case of the "Rat Man" (1909d), Freud reports what he said to the patient: "The unconscious, I explained, was the infantile; it was that part of the self which had become separated off from it in infancy, which had not shared the later stages of its development, and which had in consequence become repressed" (p. 177). A few lines previously he had equated it with the evil self. Ever since Freud's paper on "Little Hans" (1909b), child analysis has continued to develop. An extension of the field of investigation of childhood led to psychoanalysis being applied to other related disciplines—paediatrics, education, the treatment of disabled children, child psychiatry, delinquency, and more. Finally, it has been applied to observation of children and babies, something that now bears the noble name of infant research. We can consider this from two points of view. On the one hand, it may form a part of a totality embracing the themes of childhood and infancy. In such a collection, the part that is child psychoanalysis is drowned, constituting only a small part of knowledge. From the other point of view, there is a border between psychoanalysis, whether adult or child, on the one hand, and the disciplines of applied psychoanalysis in the adult or child, on the other. This second point of view is mine. I believe that there is more in common between adult and child analysis than between child analysis and infant research.

If, in 1909, Freud claimed that the infantile is the unconscious (1909d), in the rest of his work we see that infancy is not specially privileged. Other parameters come into play—for instance, the relation of the mind to the body, the relation to the "other", the role of the drives, the function of desires, wishes, fantasies, all the possible channels of representation (not limited, as usually regarded, to things and words), the conjunction of the dynamic, topographic, and economic points of view, the pleasure–unpleasure principle, the reality principle, and so on. The list is not complete—all these factors shape childhood experiences and still act throughout the person's entire life. If infant research insulates itself from all the concepts that are supposed, according to psychoanalytic thinking, to mould the events that one can consider during infancy, the theoretical result will also be insulated from psychoanalytic thinking. But are we not allowed to change our views about these concepts? Yes, but only according to the psychoanalytic setting—with or without the couch—and not only from the study of development. Moreover, we have to ask ourselves if infant research is able to provide accurate information about the other parameters we have quoted, which together contribute to delineating the specificity of our discipline. Note that I do not say our "science", as it is sometimes unwisely written.

Infant research is not qualified to be the only one that can say what the unconscious is, or the id. Its relevance or irrelevance depends on whether its objective is the specific objective of psychoanalysis: that is, neither the infant nor the child, but the unconscious. Two different issues have to be considered. The first deals with the implications of the findings of infant research on psychoanalytic theory in general. The second is the question: has infant research contributed to our knowledge of the unconscious, or the id?

Infant research, as far as psychoanalysis is concerned, arouses some confusion. It relies on methodological postulates. A major concern has been, since the time that Anna Freud remarked on it, to oppose the reconstructed child of psychoanalysis to the "real" child. In my view, as far as psychoanalysis is concerned, the "real child" is not our concern. Dialectically, I would oppose the real child to the "true" child. Where does the difference lie? The true child is based on psychic reality, a concept that has lost its original meaning. I refer here to Freud's definition of it, which rests on unconscious fantasy, dreams, and the like. Psychic reality involves the idea of an absence of doubt or of degrees of certainty. In this connection, Robert Emde and his colleagues (1997) are totally mistaken in trying to define what they call "imaginative reality". While it seems reasonable to oppose the psychic reality of the patient to external reality, in fact an analyst cannot compare the two fields, because the indications for psychoanalysis imply that the patient will not confuse the analytic setting with a torture chamber or an enchanted palace. The patient may have a fantasy that it is one, without thinking that his or her fantasy is true. It is only in the patient's unconscious that it can become true. Even when the analyst works with psychotics, the acceptance of the external reality of the setting—at least in part—is a requirement of the relationship. Even when the analyst works in institutions, he or she is not supposed to be a member of the Intelligence Service. The work of such major contributors as Wilfred Bion, Herbert Rosenfeld, Hanna Segal, and Harold Searles shows us the subtleties involved in the handling of external reality. No psychoanalyst has ever improved the condition of a psychotic patient by calling his attention to external reality and by forcing him to gain the upper hand over it. Psychoanalytic work is based on the interpretation of the patient's internal reality and of his relationships. In an analytic relationship, the real child of the past is definitely lost. What survives is a mixture of the real and the fantasized, or, to be more precise, a "reality" reshaped through fantasy.

To my mind, the efforts of Daniel Stern (1994) to "build a clinically relevant baby" are not convincing. What he is supposed to be talking about is a "clinical baby"—but what is a "clinical baby"? His efforts to build an object-related, interpersonal subjective experience make me think of an effort to build the representation of the contents of a book by observing the expressions of someone reading it, or the expressions of a couple having an unheard conversation about it. When I compare what I have written about the dead-mother complex with Stern's account of it through infant observation, I realize that nine-tenths of what I have written about is absent from Stern's comments. I suppose that he thinks that these comments of mine are irrelevant to his approach. And that is true, because he is concerned with an experimental point of view, not a clinical one. At least in regard to this issue, I am satisfied that it is adult analysis that enriches infant research, and not the other way round.

Another approach is to justify infant research from the side of epistemology. Adults show features related to childhood. Instead of speculating about childhood, we are supposed to observe children and consequently will know "what really happens there instantaneously" and what the adult patient's distortions will be. Are we not coming back to the same kind of problem that upset Freud a century ago—real seduction or fantasies of being seduced? So the question becomes: is it the patient's fantasy of his or her past or, rather, is it a true reflection of the past in the present? In this approach, no attention is paid to Winnicott's decisive contribution regarding objects that are found and created. They are found because they are already created, created because already found. But how should we explore that and construct the experiment to test the hypothesis? Many years ago, Ernst Kris (1956) raised similar questions about memories. If this discussion is still going on, we have reason to suppose that the answers have not yet convinced everyone. Childhood would be supposed to be too late for us to know exactly what the meaning of what happens is, so we would have to start from the beginning, with birth—hence infant research. We would then be able to witness the journey from beginning to end. T. S. Eliot (1943) showed us that it is not so simple, but of course he was not a scientist. The assumption of infant researchers is that if we go back to the beginning we will be able to progress from a less complex state to a more complex one (adulthood). Of course, I would raise objections about the lesser complexity of the child. We can assume that the adult is more complex because we have, at the very least, some tools that allow us to have an idea about the degree to which the adult has developed. The fact that we lack major tools for knowledge, such as language (but not only language), seems unimportant to infant researchers. If necessary, behaviour or communication through play will replace verbal communication. In fact, behaviour becomes the main point of reference. But this is not behaviourism, nor even the opposite of it, because infant researchers are concerned with building a picture of the mind, for which representation is indispensable. Stern, Emde, and Fonagy all refer to representation. The problem is that the representations they construct are less justified by scientific observation than by what I will call "science fiction", which in the present case goes together with psychoanalytic schematization. While the method of observing the facts is, I trust, respectful of scientific methodology, the inferences—as Wolff and I think—are fictions.

A criticism of Daniel Stern's ideas

I regret having to proceed to a very uncompromising criticism, based on my reading of four works by Daniel Stern. These are his well-known book, *The Interpersonal World of the Infant* (1985), and three papers—one, quoted previously, on the clinically relevant baby (1994), one on the pre-narrative envelope (1992a), and a short contribution, "Ce que comprend le bébé" [What does the baby understand?] (1995a). The two last papers appeared in French. Note that my criticism is not about the scientific nature of Stern's findings, but, rather, about the ideas that are supposed to have resulted from his experiments. I find these ideas highly speculative, in no way less so than Freud's or Melanie Klein's most unproved hypotheses; but at least the latter were born, albeit partially, "from the couch".

In his description of "pre- or proto-narrative envelopes", Stern amalgamates a number of different notions. First, Stern uses "psychic reality"—a psychoanalytic concept very specifically defined—loosely in regard to the inner world of the baby. But, of course, infant researchers are not the only ones who do this. Psychoanalysts of adults also create confusion about the notion of psychic reality, as was seen at an IPA Congress in San Francisco in 1995, where the main topic was "psychic reality". But the worst treatment inflicted on this Freudian concept was undoubtedly by Robert Emde and colleagues (1997) who showed, in their paper on "imaginative reality", a striking ignorance of Freud's ideas on the topic.

Second, Stern mixes up desire and motivation, in a strange pairing—can it be because he is attempting to build a bridge between the Freudian–Lacanian concept of desire, and the Anglo-Saxon psychological concept of motivation? What do we gain by referring to "motivation" other than to place psychoanalysis in the field of psychology? Charles Brenner (1980), with whom I am not always in agreement, says: "Just changing the name from 'drive' to say 'motivation' changes nothing in the theory. It makes the theory no more 'psychological', no less 'mechanistic', no more 'human' . . ." (p. 211).

Third, the reference to thinking, which is a concept born from modern epistemology, is also used without any precise definition although it has one in the epistemological literature (see Atlan, 1994; Varela, 1984).

Fourth, in his reference to thinking Stern does not indicate, in the slightest, to what conception of thinking he refers—Eccles? Dennett, Churchland? Davidson? Edelman? Von Foerster? Francis Crick? Nothing is said of the classical or contemporary philosophers.

Fifth, Stern mentions drives when he has to pay attention to them, perhaps because he lives in Geneva and is influenced by his French Swiss and French neighbours. In his publications in English, drives are totally absent. Instead, we have "goal-oriented experiences". Even when he talks of drives, the meanings he attributes to the drive concept have nothing to do with the psychoanalytic usage. He writes, for example, that drives generate recurring events which correspond to a schema made of internal and external episodes. Are we not closer here to the biological concept of instinct?

Sixth, Stern quotes the work of some psychoanalysts (Klein, Bion) in a way that has nothing to do with what they wrote. Bion's concept of the mother's capacity for reverie, so essential to his thinking, is in no way included in Stern's set of basic hypotheses, precisely because such a concept arose from the analytic setting and is not applicable to infant observation. Again, Bion's use of Keats's concept of negative capability—the tolerance of the unknown, and the relinquishing of forced efforts to reduce it prematurely—is alien to Stern's way of thinking. We can extend these remarks to Paul Ricoeur (1970, 1977) who has devoted his work not only to the narrative but also to the "living metaphor", and who is enlisted by Stern to support a theory of narrative envelopes in a way that is, I am afraid, alien to Ricoeur's thought.

Seventh, Stern has inferred that his aim is to describe what the baby experiences before his first experience of the world and during that experience. A "little bang", he says. In terms of speculation, this is a "bigger bang" than the boldest assumptions in astrophysics! He goes on, with the same audacity, to describe innate programmes, with their invariants and variables, and sees genetic development in a very arbitrary way. On one side we have the facts, on the other the ideas, but there are no visible links. I also find that Stern has contradictory attitudes towards the mental disposition of the researcher. At one point, Stern advises the researcher to wipe any preconception out of his mind; at another point, he recommends that the researcher put himself "in the place of the baby". He advocates achieving this identification along the lines of his hypothetical ideas, rather than on a factual basis. For Stern, others have preconceptions, but he is supposed to have none, claiming to be unprejudiced. "Empathy" is the key word. It seems to raise no problem about the accuracy of the empathy of an adult, of more than 30 years of age, with a newborn baby. Are we dealing with empathy or projection? Or even projective identification? In Peter Wolff's discussion, empathy is supposed to be evidence of the validity of infant research. A Japanese will laugh when announcing the death of a close relative, because politeness requires him not to burden one with his own sorrow. Empathy without knowing the code would induce one to think that Japanese are happy when their close relatives die. But what can one say about empathy with an infant?

Eighth, the building of representations is, for Stern, the result of "parallel distributed processing", a concept that has emerged in neurobiology. In "Ce que comprend le bébé" (1995a), he proposes a battery of six concepts, borrowed from different fields and gathered together without any substantial reason: thing and word presentations (Freud), sensorimotor schemata (Piaget), sequences, affect representations, and motivations. Representation is supposed to "emerge" from this "soup", as Stern says, referring to physics. This is also pure speculation. The anticipated scientific evidence is still to come. Is this a case of "enumerative induction"? Elsewhere he outlines six parameters: sensorimotor schemata, perceptions, concepts, scripts, temporal feeling shapes, and proto-narrative envelopes. Again a soup, but with different ingredients. My association is with the witches in Macbeth. Never mind—did not Freud call Metapsychology a witch? But at least he was conscious of the implications. The references to Freud's thing and word presentations have disappeared in this new version. As for "temporal feeling shapes" and "proto-narrative envelopes", they are Stern's inventions and not scientifically proved at all.

Ninth, in his book, *The Interpersonal World of the Infant* (1985), Stern tries to define the basis of the relationship with the "other". He says that it is not the behaviour of the person per se, "but rather some aspect of the behaviour that reflects the person's feeling state". He appears to be dealing with behaviour as expression rather than as sign or symbol: "The vehicles of transfer are metaphor and analogy." I shall come back to the relationship between metaphor and analogy. Frequently Stern's inferences make bold links between behaviourally ridden features and music, poetry, the novel, and drama. While I may feel some sympathy for his artistic tastes and share his cultural concerns, I have to discuss the so-called scientific validity of his ideas, which is far from being tested.

Last, but not least, tenth: in Stern's formulations, just as in those of other infant researchers, there is an inflation of an ad hoc terminology. One of the most striking examples is the use of the prefixes "pre" or "proto", which have dozens of applications. Thus we hear of pre-objects, genetic pre-structure, pre-thinking, proto-narrative, predetermined epigenesis. I have quoted only a few. The sleight of hand here consists of adding a prefix to a term, the newly created term being supposed to help us understand a particular outcome, result, or consequence by referring to its antecedent. In fact, the outcome is already worded in the antecedent. For instance, we do not know what a pre-object is except that it will become an object. How? Through what type of transformation? We receive no answer. Thus it is the object that helps in defining the pre-object, and not the reverse. If one is in trouble about defining something, one simply adds "pre-" or "proto-". In Freudian metapsychology, the prefix that has a privileged position is "re" (the return of), as in "representation", which implies that we know the workings of the mind better when we witness the reappearance of something after it had disappeared, in a form different from the way it first appeared. This involves a new theory of perception, which is still under examination on the basis of clinical findings, as Freud's theory is in this respect inadequate and insufficient, on the basis of our clinical findings.

So what does infant research amount to? The answer is that there has been considerable progress about knowledge of infancy considered from the angle of consciousness. This is the outcome of studies of the relationship between the infant and its important figures—the "psychoanalytically informed" researchers, who should not be confused with psychoanalysts. As Bion once said: "It is very easy to look like a psychoanalyst, and very difficult to be one." What of the researcher who no longer calls the parent of the infant the love object, but rather the "caregiver"? Do caregivers have sexual desires, do they love, do they hate, do they have fantasies, do they dream—who cares? I find myself in agreement with Wolff that it is an abuse of language to speak of the subjective experience of the infant. The inferences here are unlimited. The clinical situation does not pretend to be a scientific setting. The inferences made by the analyst are known and the analyst knows that he is constructing the patient's mind more than he is reconstructing the patient's infancy. As psychoanalysts, our true object is not the infant but the infant in the adult, which may have very little to do with the question of what really happened to the patient in infancy. Then what about the infant in the infant? If one has to deal with a child, there is "an infant in the child". If it is an infant that is being investigated, then the researcher's postulates, beliefs, and methods are part of that person's understanding of infancy through the adult that he or she is, and even (why not?) his or her own infancy. This is why we have so many conceptions of infancy, none of which is considered as being universally true, nor having the right to falsify the others. Who is right—Freud, Melanie Klein, Bion, Winnicott, Anna Freud, Hartmann, the Sandlers, Lebovici? Apart from Freud, all the others have been able to understand something about infants and children because they have been previously analysed. There is more in common in these divergent theories than between any of them and Stern's, Emde's, or Fonagy's. The enormous scientific apparatus of infant research cannot hide the paucity of its significance. The gap between the facts and the ideas is no less than in Melanie Klein's most fantastic speculations. As Wolff says, hypotheses have to be verified. Finally, the results look more like science fiction than science, except that they are less imaginative.

In the end, what is the aim of infant researchers? It is clear that, after one has read the best of their papers, what they are trying to do is to destroy psychoanalytic theory—in fact, all psychoanalytic theories built on any other basis than research—and to replace them by a non-psychoanalytic, so-called scientific psychology, with which they are more at ease, because it is more simple, more amenable to experimental studies, and easier to teach.

Metapsychology and empirical research: metaphor squashed

It would be wrong to think that infant research is a recent vogue. Emmanuel Peterfreund (1978) launched a strong attack on psychoanalytic conceptualizations of infancy. For instance, he criticized Margaret Mahler's (Mahler et al., 1975) work, and expressed the view that poor analysts may have been led to believe that with the results of her researches they were growing scientifically. This sort of criticism will become increasingly severe as time goes by. At one point or another, the scientific approach in psychoanalysis will have to cope with metaphor. Metaphor usually receives poor treatment in these research approaches, and Peterfreund (1978) reduces it to analogy. Roman Jakobson (1990) would surely be surprised. Peterfreund's analogies are "simple", he says, and he expresses the same prejudice against the increasing complexity of the attributes of the infant. However, the most astonishing thing is that he thinks that he addresses the "subjective experiences" of his theoretical child, whom he names "Theo". God's name (p. 431)? His constructed child is more like a robot or a computer than a human being, and its so-called psychic life is a total abstraction. It is surprising how much Peterfreund thinks he knows about an infant. In fact, he is not observing an infant, but is, rather, making one. Much of what is, and will be, opposed to the truly psychoanalytic concepts of the infant have their source here—there is a refutation of the undifferentiated phase, infantile narcissism, omnipotence, hallucinatory wish-fulfilment, and the stimulus barrier. These notions do not fit the perspective of observation. How right he is—except that psychoanalysis is incompatible with observation. Observation cannot tell us anything about intrapsychic processes that truly characterize the subject's experience. Objectivism cannot be changed into subjectivism without denying what it wants to replace.

Peterfreund's ferocious attack against many psychoanalytic concepts is part of the systematic demolition of Freud's metapsychology, a demolition that has never ceased and is going on to the present day, mostly in the United States. What Peterfreund aims at is not even a psychology—rather, it is a biological theory of the mind. Since 1978 we have had many opportunities to witness the impasses brought about by such a view. It seems that psychoanalysis has to be either a psychological or a biological theory, but for Freud it is neither the one nor the other. If some psychoanalysts cannot use metapsychology, that is their problem. Perhaps they should read those who think they can make use of it, and who make the effort to understand the problems that underlie it. But this would need an extension of the reading lists of the psychoanalysts and of the "psychoanalytically informed" researchers. Peterfreund is an extreme example of simplistic pseudo-psychoanalytic reductionism. "When a complex machine breaks down it rarely retraces the problems by which it was formed and one must be very careful in drawing inferences about the construction of the machine from observation of its products of breakdown. Likewise, when a complex biological system breaks down . . ." (p. 439). It is interesting to note that many of Peterfreund's criticisms will be accepted by infant researchers (e.g., the non-existence of the undifferentiated phase, or the origin of the ego). He clearly states (p. 440) that "meaningful psychoanalytic theories of infancy will not emerge from the current metapsychology but from different frames of reference—neurophysiological, biological, genetic, evolutionary, and informational—all of which are consistent with one another" (and inconsistent with psychoanalytic experience!).

Metapsychology and empirical research: metaphor restored

> A . . . plausible reason for the distant relationship between empirical and theoretical studies might be the poor knowledge of psychoanalytic theory on the part of investigators. Unfortunately, most validational experimental studies, whether out of oversimplification, inadequate formulation or unfamiliarity, ignore the function and falsify the content of the psychoanalytic concepts under investigation. [Fonagy, 1982, p. 129]

Fonagy here expresses the opinions of Edelson (1977). Observational techniques are evidently not so reliable, as Fonagy himself notices, for he says that "observational techniques, however, have inherent limitations which often coincide with those of appraisal within the clinical setting" (p. 128). However, he does not mention that in the clinical setting language is an invaluable source of information. But Fonagy has the hope that modern techniques have overcome the shortcomings of earlier attempts. He also writes "Thus the experimental verification of psychoanalytic theory might not be a meaningful endeavour" (p. 129). It seems that years later these sceptical remarks have been wiped out, repressed, or foreclosed. Nevertheless, the central debate is metapsychology versus empirical research. Central to this is the unavoidable question of metaphor.

The critiques of metapsychology come from everywhere—from infant research and from clinical analysts as well as from enemies of psychoanalysis such as M. Borch-Jacobsen (1988). Step by step we have now reached an almost zero level of metapsychology with the advent of the intersubjectivists in the United States. I wonder if French analysts who still believe in metapsychology have retarded minds. It could be so.

Fonagy, like Peterfreund, has to come to metaphor, except that he does not equate it with analogy. And, at last, he also arrives at language. He writes (1982): "Fonagy [without giving the person's first name] in a monograph concerning the use of metaphor in the history of phonetics, outlined its significance in the development of modern phonology" (p. 135). This refers to Ivan Fonagy, Peter Fonagy's caregiver, whom I have the privilege of knowing personally. "It is a fascinating fact that European grammarians of the sixteenth to eighteenth centuries, under Hellenic influence developed a classification system of phonemes using metaphors, strikingly similar to independent systems developed by Mongols, Chinese and Sanskrit grammarians" (Fonagy, 1982, p. 135). It is surely a valid and fascinating problem, of a non-hermeneutic nature, but not positivistic either. Its importance lies in the fact that phonemes are the minimal elements of language, devoid of meaning but having meaningful relationships that form the basis of structural linguistics. Here we meet the *"fort–da"* game, in which the baby pronounces *"o-o-o-o da"*.[1] The interplay of phonemes is still present in poetics (see the work of Roman Jakobson, who wrote the preface to Ivan Fonagy's 1983 work *La vive voix* [The Living Voice]). Ivan Fonagy has demonstrated the presence of drives in phonation. But, at last, I can come to an agreement with the 1982 version of Peter Fonagy when he writes: "Metaphors in metapsychology may be thought of as representing attempts on the part of the theorists to grasp the nature of the psychological processes and mechanisms of which we have no conscious knowledge and which are not available to introspection" (p. 136). I agree, and wish to conclude this section by quoting him once again: "The empirical basis of psychoanalysis is the clinical situation. The laboratory does not provide its empirical base and as the theory is not based on laboratory findings it cannot be either disproved or validated on them" (p. 138). Moreover, he adds that the laboratory findings have "very limited applications" (p. 139). Again, I agree.

[1] *Editorial note*: The game referred to here was recounted by Freud in *Beyond the Pleasure Principle* (1920g). Freud described a well-behaved little boy of one-and-a-half, who never cried when his mother left him alone for some hours, although he was very attached to her. When left alone he frequently threw small objects from his bed, at the same time uttering a loud and drawn-out *"o-o-o-o"*. His mother and Freud agreed that this represented the German word *"fort"* [gone]. Freud writes: "One day I made an observation which confirmed my view. The child had a wooden reel with a piece of string tied round it. . . . What he did was to hold the reel by the string and very skilfully throw it over the edge of his curtained cot, so that it disappeared into it, at the same time uttering an expressive '*o-o-o-o*'. He then pulled the reel out of the cot again by the string and hailed its reappearance with a joyful '*da*' [there]. This, then, was the complete game—disappearance and return" (p. 15).

The child and the dream

What is the paradigm for psychoanalytic thinking? What guarantees the maintenance of the psychoanalytic state of mind I am advocating? Here a basic choice is presented. As I wrote in 1979, it is either the child or the dream that has the role as the central point of reference. In my opinion, those who have believed that the answers would only come from childhood took the wrong path. But sometimes we have surprises. After Melanie Klein, Bion is the only Kleinian who obviously opted for the dream, rather than for the child. And even Winnicott (1971), who contributed so greatly to our knowledge of the infant and the child, states in his *Therapeutic Consultations*, where he uses the "squiggle game", that the most important moment of the consultation—in fact its target—is when the child is ready to recount a dream; but, through research, we only know of the infant's dream what the electroencephalogram will tell us. The dream model is of cardinal importance because we only know *après coup* (*nachträglich*) what has been important during the day previous to the session and which escaped our attention—an evanescent fantasy, which has been repressed, sorted out through the dream work into latent thoughts and returning to consciousness through secondary revision, into a manifest content artificially narrated. It is exactly the same with childhood—one only knows what has been really important, from the point of view of the unconscious, in the analysis of the transference, or, as the Sandlers (1983) would say, through investigating the present unconscious. Any method that aims at following, step by step, the stages of the building of the "Self" is bound to result in misunderstanding as far as the unconscious is concerned.

In 1925, in the preface to Aichhorn's *Wayward Youth*, Freud writes:

> The possibility of analytic influence rests on quite definite preconditions which can be summed up under the term "analytic situation"; it requires the development of certain psychical structures and a particular attitude to the analyst. Where these are lacking—as in the case of children . . . something other than analysis must be employed. . . . [1925f, pp. 274]

He implicitly admits that the reference is to the adult in the analytic setting. Of course, the *Three Essays on the Theory of Sexual-*

ity (1905d) were partially the result of observation. Nevertheless, Freud's idea of science (and we know that he thought that psychoanalysis was a science) was not to give up some of his hypotheses even in the many instances where they blatantly contradicted the scientific facts. This conception of science, which looks like a manifesto, has nothing to do with our present methodology. Yet Freud's remarks as an observer are matched with speculations that are now denied. For instance, Daniel Stern says that there is no oral phase. Therefore, Freud's idea of "leaning" (*Anlehnung*)[2]—the leaning of sexual drives on self-preservative ones—falls away, just as do many other hypotheses that are omitted from discussion. We heard at the International Psychoanalytical Association Congress held in Barcelona in 1997 that "we have reached beyond that" in relation to sexuality. In what respect? What about the erotogenic zones? There is little interest in them in infant research. What about masturbation, and, finally, is the child still polymorphously perverse? I suggest that the second of the *Three Essays* (Freud, 1905d) be reread to see how far we have travelled in discovering new continents: object relations, the now defunct Ego Psychology, all kinds of "Selves" from Hartmann to Kohut, as well as aggression, and, where we have now arrived, with triumphant intersubjectivity.

Good-enough observation and imaginative concepts

Am I denying the importance of observing children? That would also be irrelevant. Fonagy rightly recalls Freud's writing about the *"fort–da"* game, a game that has been reinterpreted after Freud by many psychoanalysts, from Susan Isaacs to Lacan, with different interpretations, including my own. More recently, Emde et al. (1997) added their comments on psychic reality to the voluminous literature about the concept, which I have no time to discuss here.

[2] *Editorial note*: In the English *Standard Edition*, the German *Anlehnung* has been translated as "anaclitic". Nowadays, the terms "dependent" and "dependence" would be more appropriate.

How can they write about the *"fort–da"* game that "What is less appreciated is that Freud presented us with observations of an early form of pretence in terms making use of an alternate form of symbolic reality" (p. 119) when this is precisely the core of Lacan's interpretation of the game, except that Lacan goes very much beyond pretence? (Emde has the same point of view regarding the application of psychological ideas.) Pretence in children has been known since Aristotle's Poetics.

The richness of Freud's contribution lies in its having enhanced multiple interpretations, just like a masterpiece of literature. I want to add to this the significant contribution of Winnicott, which I strongly support and admire, to child and infant observation. For ages before Winnicott, paediatricians and psychoanalysts witnessed the child holding its teddy bear tightly or sucking its piece of blanket, but no one had had the idea of concepts such as those of the transitional object, transitional phenomena, and transitional space, which by definition are not observable. In Emde et al. (1997) there are quotations of stunning criticisms of Winnicott's concept of the transitional. These authors argue that Winnicott's concepts are metaphors—regarded as a sin, for they "lack coherence and have since become idealised and over-generalised" (p. 126). Emde shares these criticisms and is in favour of a "continual form of mental life" (p. 126). Wallerstein also defended a similar idea in his argument against me in his discussion in chapter two. What this means is that the radical opposition between the conscious/preconscious and the unconscious is denied. It seems that those who plead for genetic continuity know only the preconscious, not the unconscious. Their perspective is phenomenological rather than psychoanalytical.

No infant researcher could have discovered the concepts of projective identification or of reparation, which were drawn from the couch. No infant researcher had the slightest idea of an "alpha function" nor even of a capacity for reverie in the mother. *A fortiori*, Bion's grid (1963) is absolutely out of the question for an experimentalist. I quote these concepts because they have widely proved how fertile they are, even outside the borders of the subgroup in which they were born. Psychoanalysts all over the world have recognized in them ideas that illuminate their experiences with their patients. If it does not fit the laboratory, *tant pis*—too bad—

for the laboratory, for superficial findings, and for simplistic ideas. We can survive their loss.

What I am arguing against is the adequacy of so-called scientific "method" which seems to me very unscientific because of its irrelevance to the object of psychoanalysis. I would suggest the following experiment to infant researchers: take twenty-five or fifty 18-month-old babies who have been in the absence of their mothers and keep them in their beds, each with a cotton reel attached to a string. Observe them, video-tape them, do whatever you want to record what they do, and draw your conclusions from this statistical evidence. For observers whose minds are not fit to think, the observations will provide them with nothing. If children whose behaviours are qualitatively different are studied, the researchers will get nothing. But imagine another situation. Suppose you show the film of the child's activity with the cotton reel, as Freud described it, to an imaginary meeting of child observers such as Spitz, Mahler, Lebovici, Winnicott, Emde, Fonagy, and Stern, who are, for this hypothetical situation, supposed to know nothing of Freud's comments. Then collect their observations. I would wager that we will not hear two analogous answers. The reply of the infant researchers would be: "That's why we have to do it scientifically." In doing it scientifically, how far are they from the analytic setting? How far will their remarks enlighten the specificity of the psychoanalytic approach? How close will they be to our fundamental rule—that is, to free association and its correspondence in the analyst's mind, evenly suspended attention? How free will they feel to interpret? One major objection regarding infant research made by Peter Wolff was the neglect of the free-association method of clinical psychoanalysis, which he considered to be of major importance and incompatible with the findings based on an ordinated sequence of events. Very few discussants took up this point in their controversy with Wolff.

At times, the findings of psychological science are supposed to enlighten situations met with by psychoanalysis. A very popular concept coming from psychological findings, and applied to psychoanalysis, is the notion of the representation of the mind of the other. Fonagy and Emde make wide use of the notion. For instance, Emde et al. (1997, p. 126) propose to refer to "psychic reality in terms of what is meaningful subjective experience that can be known by another because of its expression"—a typical example of psychological reductionism. Several remarks need to be made here, quite apart from reference to Emde's very peculiar conception of psychic reality, as it has a meaning opposite to what was meant by Freud.

1. First, a comment on the theory of mind, which is very fashionable nowadays. The reference to the other's mind is present in Freud's paper "The Unconscious" (1915e):

   > Consciousness makes each of us aware only of his own states of mind; that other people, too, possess a consciousness is an inference we draw by analogy from their observable utterances and actions in order to make this behaviour of theirs intelligible to us. (It would no doubt be psychologically more correct to put it this way: that without any special reflection we attribute to everyone else our own constitution and therefore our consciousness as well, and that this identification is sine qua non of our understanding.) [p. 169]

2. The modern concept of the theory of mind arose from the experience of work with autistic children. It is an inference derived from a pathological state and transferred to normal infancy. This contradicts the claim of the infant researchers that it is not right to apply the findings of pathology to normality.
3. The mechanism as observed in autism is contradicted by many other findings. For example, there is the work of Frances Tustin (1981, 1988) and, more recently, of J.-M. Vidal (1993), who has shown its limited value, emphasizing in his own findings the role of the refusal of "thirdness" (Green, 1979).

In my debate with Robert Wallerstein (see part I), I tried to show how the procedures of research (even if those involved were adults who had experienced a psychoanalysis) were inadequate because they were not applicable to the type of mental functioning of the patient in the analytic session, and with the corresponding state of mind of the analyst listening to the free association of the patient with his free-floating attention. The analyst deciphers the unconscious meaning of the patient's associations, at times in the succession of sentences, and at other times in a non-chronological order, to and fro, in the sequence of a discourse which is the contrary of narrative. The concept of narrative truth, put forward by Donald Spence (1982), is also inadequate. Patients do not tell us stories, but sometimes use stories to say something else. For most of the time, during their narrative they resist the analytic process. I have described a type of discourse that I called *"narratif–récitatif"* (narrative-recitative) as typical of narcissistic patients defending themselves against transference and against free association. The narrative is only in the analyst's mind, which tries to put some order into the required disorder of thought of the patient. The analyst is not only compelled to construct the past as it is in the mind of the patient, but also the processes—primary, secondary, and tertiary (Green, 1986b)—in the current analytic situation. The concept of tertiary processes is one of my own, used to explain the linking processes occurring between the primary and secondary ones. We would do better by returning to Freud's notion of historical truth, which has so often been confused with truth drawn from the chronology of history.

Thanks to the scientific method, and to ideas born of speculation more than from scientific evidence, it is possible to arrive at very interesting findings. However, these will, in my opinion, have very little to do with psychoanalysis. It is true that not all interesting findings are necessarily connected with psychoanalytic theory. But what is interesting is not what we are searching for. Rather, we try to find the most useful explanatory hypotheses about the way the human mind functions in regard to its specific forms of disorganization.

Past and present

I agree, on many points, with Joseph and Anne-Marie Sandler (1983, 1994) about the distinction between past and present unconscious. But the new findings about memory do not, in principle, affect Freud's conceptions, a topic that needs a long explanation. It is not enough to exult and shout: "Ah! The old man was wrong, it is scientifically proven." We have to ask ourselves what the connection is between his speculations—which may be rejected by contemporary science—and the central object of the discipline he created. What are the underlying epistemological problems that even he did not always spell out? Like the Sandlers, I also think that the "templates" of the past unconscious are internal structures that unconsciously orientate later experiences. We carry within ourselves the totality of our past, which does not mean that we carry it as memories but as a set of organizers.

We have to remember, again and again, that the specific task of psychoanalysis is the analysis of intrapsychic work, either in a subjective way or through the intersubjective relationship. But we should not forget that an intersubjective experience or an object relationship or "being with the other", as Stern says, necessarily connects two intrapsychic structures anchored both in the unconscious and in bodies. I am afraid that Bowlby's (1969, 1973, 1980) concept of attachment has blinded some minds. He seems to be at the root of the "scientific" movement. All infant researchers refer to attachment. But what about Bowlby's contributions to psychoanalytic experience? Here we can note the difference between Bowlby on the one hand, and Winnicott, Bion, and Klein, on the other. And, with regard to intersubjectivity, we need to answer the question: "What is a subject?" If we find little help in philosophy, especially in the so-called philosophy of mind, we may turn to the latest discovery of epistemology—hypercomplexity—which I am afraid will be satisfied neither with the procedures nor the conclusions of infant research.

Three generations in femininity

It is time to give clinical material in order to provide a less theoretical type of evidence.

> A young mother, aged 32, daughter of a psychoanalyst and having psychotherapy herself at the time of the incident I shall describe, is pregnant, expecting a second, very much wished-for baby. The pregnancy was kept secret early on because of an earlier pregnancy that had ended in a miscarriage after two

months. This had occurred a few months previously and was not disclosed. Two-and-a-half months after the beginning of the present pregnancy, feeling that she was less available and receptive to her 20-month-old daughter, she was worried—very understandably—about her condition. Also—but this belongs to my own thoughts, as I was an occasional observer of the situation—the fact that she was reluctant to carry her daughter in her arms now because of the risk of another abortion echoed a situation that had existed six months before the present pregnancy, when her daughter was 14 months old. At that time, the mother had her foot operated on and was on crutches and not able to carry the baby for some time, worrying more about the effect on the baby's mind than about her own condition. She was concerned about the effect of all this on her relationship to her daughter, as the latter could not at all understand the reason for not being carried during the convalescence of the mother. I should like to draw attention to the correspondence in the mother's mind of the "miscarriage". She finally decided, for practical reasons, to make her pregnancy known, and started this with her daughter by saying to her: "You know, we are going to have a baby." The child shouted "Baby, baby" and walked around the house in search of a child, a reaction the mother immediately understood. The little girl was looking for a small child with whom she used to play, who together with his parents had been staying as guests of the family, but had recently returned home. So the mother then said to her daughter, "No, the baby is here", showing her belly, which at that time showed no perceptible change. The girl then went to her room to take one of her dolls and put it on the mother's belly.

After about an hour, the mother realized that the child had disappeared. Trying to find her, the mother discovered her hidden in a closet, sucking her thumb, an activity that she had given up. The mother said to her, "What are you doing here?" and asked her daughter to come out of the closet. The child then asked to have her dummy (comforter), which she had completely abandoned a long time before, and put it in her mouth in place of her thumb. She then kept the dummy in her mouth all day long, even when she ate, taking it out only to let food come in, putting it back in her mouth even when she chewed her food. The next day she continued to play in the closet, but she would ask her mother to come with her into that dark space.

I was, as I said, an occasional observer. I could have my thoughts about the situation because the mother of the mother—the grandmother of the child—was herself a psychoanalyst. She told me about it because she had been struck by what had happened. The narrative was completed by her daughter, the child's mother. The grandmother also told me that the child's mother was now exactly the same age as she was when expecting her third child (the daughter being the second).

The "associations"—or, as I call them, "mnemic reverberations"—can never be derived from a single observation of the child. Not only do we know nothing about the child's subjective experience if we are content with generalities of minor importance or behavioural features; the latter may give us the illusion that we understand something while in fact we are completely misguided by what we think we have understood, for we lack information about what it is, in the mind of the child, that lies behind its behaviour. All sorts of problems arise about memory, fantasy, regression, sexual curiosity, and the like.

A last word about psychoanalytic epistemology

What epistemological strategy can help to answer these questions? I have to confess that my thinking here is indebted to Freud, Melanie Klein, Bion, and Winnicott, and not in the slightest to the "psychoanalytically informed" infant researchers. It is not so much that psychoanalytic concepts must come from the couch, but rather that they must refer to the analytic setting, as the setting is a polysemic metaphor; it includes reference to the model of the dream, to incestuous prohibition, and to maternal care, all of these condensed, one with the other. In all cases, it provides an opportunity to observe and participate in a unique form of mental functioning, which is the only way through which the analytic state of mind can be experienced, integrated, and tested, year after year, day after day, hour after hour. Here, observation takes on an entire different meaning, because it is nourished not with the eyes, but with the ears. Even two ears are not enough; a third, as everyone knows, is required.

CHAPTER FIVE

The relevance of empirical infant research to psychoanalytic theory and practice

Daniel N. Stern

This presentation consists of two sections. First, I discuss some of the major epistemological differences that bear on whether one thinks that infant observation is relevant to psychoanalysis. I will address my comments largely to André Green, whose position I have some familiarity with from our several meetings and his various publications and public interviews on this subject.

Second, I describe some of the specific differences in approach between infant observation and psychoanalysis. This will include a discussion of how an observer of infants might view some issues that are central to psychoanalysis, but quite differently. My intention in so doing is to push forward the dialogue about relevance and possible complementarity.

Epistemological differences between the psychoanalytic and infant observational approaches

To begin, we need to examine what is meant by "relevance". That is the key word.

First, is empirical infant observation *directly* relevant to psychoanalysis? I agree with André Green that infant observations can never prove or disprove a clinical or theoretical tenet of psychoanalysis. Their epistemological differences do not permit a defining encounter. Scientific "truth" and psychoanalytic coherence, concerning meta-theory or clinical reconstruction, cannot directly challenge one another. Only if, or when, psychoanalysis proposes a specific or general predictive hypothesis can science, as a method of hypothesis testing, become directly relevant in the sense of confirming or disconfirming the prediction. Psychoanalysis, in the main, does not engage in this kind of prediction, nor does it have to. In fact, such predictions and hypotheses are thought by most psychoanalysts to be outside the psychoanalytic discourse. This is both an advantage and disadvantage.

So, accepting this view of the nature and specificity of psychoanalysis, the answer is "No"—infant observation is not directly relevant. Associated with this, the observer being a psychoanalyst, and even having his or her questions inspired by psychoanalytic issues, does not make the interpretations of his or her observations, *per se*, "psychoanalytic", in the sense of being directly relevant.

Second, there is the far more crucial and interesting question: can infant observation be *indirectly* relevant to psychoanalysis? What do I mean by indirect relevance? There is a small but vital interface where an encounter does take place between psychoanalysis and infant observation. If we view psychoanalysis as a theory, or as a systematic narrative, and view clinical reconstructions as personal theories, one of the criteria of the "validity" of a theory or narrative, besides coherence, parsimony, comprehensibility, elegance, and so forth, is its plausibility. Is the metapsychology or clinical reconstruction plausible?

Plausibility necessarily concerns what we know in general, outside psychoanalysis, about the world and, for our purposes here, about human psychological development. Infant observations continue to add enormously to our general knowledge about aspects of who a baby is, and what are possible and what unlikely hypotheses, theories, and narratives about them. World knowledge provides the background and basis of plausibility, and it exists external to psychoanalysis.

Plausibility can place considerable doubts or constraints on what is an acceptable psychoanalytic notion, be it theoretical or clinical. These doubts are not the result of a direct challenge. As Ricoeur (1977) points out, plausibility is the point at which the hermeneutic circle of psychoanalysis must open and make contact with other domains of knowledge or speculation—in this case, infant development. This is the form of indirect relevance that concerns us here. While indirect, it nonetheless may carry much force. This is so because, while the tenets of psychoanalysis are epistemologically protected from scientific "truths", they are, like any theory, open and sensitive to doubts, perplexing difficulties, potential boundaries, and limiting conditions. And perhaps the greatest source of these doubts is plausibility. A broad intellectual interest in psychoanalysis ultimately rests on this pillar of its relationship and fit with the rest of our current world knowledge. When this relatedness is broken or becomes too weakened, the psychoanalytic discourse stops being interesting and gets left behind—not because it is wrong or right, but because it has lost contact and import for the rest of the intellectual culture. For instance, the existence of a "normal autistic phase" is simply not plausible in light of the findings of infant observation. This research does not disprove the existence of such a phase. However, it does act to isolate this particular psychoanalytic tenet from the mainstream of general knowledge and thus makes its acceptability precarious.

Third, how important can this form of indirect relevance be? That is very hard to answer. Doubts, perplexities, difficulties, and limitations coming indirectly can bring down the whole theoretical house, or they can lead to modifications, or they can have no impact at all, depending on the reading. I have mostly argued for modifications and, in some cases, serious reappraisals in psychoanalytic thinking that reduce the doubts and implausibilities revealed by *indirect* evidence.

Fourth, does infant observation have a privileged role as a source of indirect relevance, in comparison, say, to literature, anthropology, mythology, and so on? André Green would say "no". When it concerns the developmental aspects of psychoanalysis, I would say, "yes, of course". This yes would include the psychoanalytic developmental psychology(ies) that have accumulated over the years. After all, psychoanalysis has evolved one of the most influential developmental psychologies, one that continues to touch many fields. It would also include the development suppositions that help each analyst to structure individual, clinical reconstructions. I would say "no" to a privileged role when it concerned the other non-developmental aspects of psychoanalysis. This seems self-evident.

The fifth point concerns a disagreement about the nature and spirit of infant observation, and science in general, as contrasted to that of psychoanalysis. André Green has frequently argued that observational research and experimental research—that is, systematic research, based on overt behaviour, using large numbers of subjects, and producing statistical results applicable only to groups—are meaningless for psychoanalysis. He then goes further and characterizes infant observational work like mine as pseudo-neutral, pseudo-scientific, and against what he calls "the spirit of psychoanalysis" and therefore irrelevant. I will take up each of these. But first it is necessary to clarify that there are many modes of science. They cannot all be lumped together and dismissed as one. Perhaps the most pertinent distinction is between science that is hypothesis generating, as against hypothesis testing.

A slight detour will best make my point. When I first began to use cine-film to help observe mother–infant interactions, it was not to measure anything, nor to be a more precise behaviourist (which I never was anyway). Nor was it to see naively, as if that were possible. It was to use all my preconceptions, idiosyncrasies, and intuitions to *see* differently, if possible, and describe what I saw, because existing descriptions ("explanations")—psychoanalytic and others—of what happened between young infants and the parents seemed unsatisfactory and inadequate. To see what? To see how, from observing the form and timing of the interaction, I could imagine—and I emphasize the word imagine—the infant's subjective world, and how conceivably the infant could represent its relational world. The initial work was conducted on one single case of twins.

The first step was to explore how the mother–infant interaction could be viewed and described. The descriptions that emerged, however, had to be helpful from the perspective of this question: "What might the infant's experience be like from his point of view? And how could this be represented?" This perspective seemed a necessary place to start. Trying to position yourself inside the baby's mind is more speculative, even fictional, than scientific and constitutes a perspective that initially does not have its centre of gravity in psychoanalytic theory, nor in empirical scientific method. I did not measure anything for a long while; rather, I brought together a group of choreographers and stage directors who were, like me, starting out and were doing "experimental" theatre and dance. For a year or so we worked together: once a month we watched my films, and the next month we would go to one of their studios to watch their work in progress. The common point concerned how to describe the form and timing of movements and sounds that are emotionally evocative. For instance, what happens affectively and cognitively when motion is slowed down, when it is held frozen, or accelerated, when it is performed backwards; how one could unpack the phraseology of a gesture and learn how a movement contour evokes the audience's affective reaction; what the emotional aspects are of moving together in strict synchrony, in loose synchrony, or in turns, and so forth. All of these and many other such questions apply to babies and parents as well as to the theatre.

After a while of doing this, I switched into the scientific-empirical stance, performing frame-by-frame film measurements. But for me, the value of the observations was already largely accomplished: my view of the baby's world was changed, the direction of the empirical observations that followed were reoriented, and the nature of the measurements made was shifted. The quantitative results could only capture a small part of the imaginings that stimulated them; they did not necessarily verify or confirm them, they simply added to their plausibility.

So now I shall return to André Green's criticisms, the first being that infant observational research is pseudo-neutral. He is partly right, but for the wrong reasons, and he comes up with the wrong conclusions, as does Peter Wolff (1996) on whom Green has unfortunately relied too heavily and uncritically. André Green and others act as if they do not realize that the kind of wide-ranging reflection, introspection, and exposure to various human experiences that I just described must necessarily precede quantitative research, where the aim is to generate hypotheses not to test them. This distinction is crucial.

The first step in such hypothesis-generating observational work is pattern recognition. This requires something like evenly hovering attention not so different from the efforts of pattern recognition required for the clinical material of psychoanalysis. Pattern recognition in movement and sound, remember, babies are pre-verbal, just as pattern recognition for meanings, is initially an art, requiring a great deal of the observer. It requires participation, empathic immersion, projection, and introspection by the observer in order to come up with his or her own intuitive sense of what he or she thinks is happening.

The next step is a confirmation/disconfirmation step, or, in its weaker form, a plausibility check. In psychoanalysis, the interpretation-as-hypothesis is the confirmation/plausibility step. After all, what is being checked out in an interpretation is not only the validity of the content, but also the correctness of the timing. In developmental research, using the example of the cine-film research above, the confirmation/plausibility check was the controlled, quantitative frame-by-frame analysis. In both the psychoanalytic and the infant-observation situation, either the initial intuition is strengthened, but rarely definitively verified, or it is weakened; in the latter case, one is thrown back into the intuitive mode, but with the advantage of having the checking process to stimulate new reflections. In other words, infant research, or any research carried out in this way, cannot be dismissed as pseudo-neutral science. It is a legitimate discourse or discipline that yokes an intuitive, subjective procedure with a scientific method in a recursive dialogue. This kind of hypothesis-generating inquiry is a discourse just as psychoanalysis is.

So, it is not pseudo-neutral, but is it pseudo-scientific as Green and Wolff also claim? This question has to do with the tightness of the fit between the questions asked, the adequacy of the methods used to answer, and the level of the interpretation—and whether the aim is to arrive at truths or hypotheses. The reason that certain infant observational research runs into some trouble here is that the questions that are being asked—such as, what is the baby experiencing?—can have no satisfactory method for responding fully. The question, however, is unavoidable. The interpretations that are linked to the questions thus make a leap unjustified by the logical-empirical system of science used for hypothesis testing. This happens exactly because the questions are the tough ones inspired by crucial clinical concerns—that is, where a more rigorous and narrow posing of the problem loses the essence of the question. One can only make progressive approximations towards answering such questions. André Green and Peter Wolff seem to want to restrict infant research to the narrow questions where available methodology can definitively test hypotheses. The infancy research of greatest interest to psychoanalysis does not lie there, but rather in hypothesis generation.

Here is how I proceed with this endeavour. The questions and suppositions come from psychoanalytic and other theories, personal experience, and other sources. Armed, or contaminated (if you prefer), with these questions and notions, I have an encounter with the doings of babies and their parents—that is, with clinical material, though not psychoanalytic material to be sure. It is important to note that very few psychoanalytic thinkers have made extensive observations of young infants. They do not know the material at first hand, which is a devastating limitation. Winnicott is the most striking exception. Margaret Mahler is only a partial exception because she rarely observed infants under a year of age. We are already agreed that observing babies is not a psychoanalytic enterprise, but it is the essential enterprise for accumulating knowledge that is potentially of indirect relevance.

To return to the encounter with babies, it takes place under very special rules. The observations that emerge and their interpretation are guided by and must respect— but not be blinded by—the constraints imposed by the current state of accepted, accumulated, scientific knowledge about babies. Peter Wolff and André Green overlook these rules. So, while my inferences are speculations, they are not pure fictions because they have been deeply informed and constrained by an established context. And they are not circular, because the starting point and certain constraints have been externally established by others—that is, by the world community of developmentalists. I consider this procedure acceptable for hypothesis generation, not for hypothesis testing. Accordingly, I am not talking about scientific truths but about productive hypotheses. And I am describing a form of discourse to arrive there—and there are not many other discourses for so doing.

This leaves the question of the "psychoanalytic spirit" that André Green insists upon. I fail to see the difference between the nature of the psychoanalytic discourse—that is, its assumptions, questions, methods, and so forth—and what André Green calls the "psychoanalytic spirit". The psychoanalytic discourse runs into the same problems of the questions and methods determining the possible discoveries and their likely interpretation. The notion of a "psychoanalytic spirit" simply mystifies an already complex issue.

To summarize, André Green oversimplifies the debate to cast it in terms of pseudo-science versus science, or in terms of psychoanalysis versus any kind of science. The real question is whether the legitimate discourse of hypothesis generation in infant observation which I have just described has anything of interest to say to the psychoanalytic discourse, and vice-versa. I am speaking of indirect relevance.

Some areas of possible indirect relevance and complementarity

Because the baby is preverbal and pre-symbolic, and most of what there is to observe is action or interaction, infant observers are lead and forced to think up different kinds of questions, even when these are inspired by the same psychoanalytic issues that concern adults. And there is often the advantage of having to go to the very beginning of a question, starting at zero, where one encounters the need to re-examine what had been taken for granted or to view it quite differently. This offers certain freedoms.

With the above in mind, I will consider several issues shared in common: the nature of "raw" experience, its representation, and its intersubjectivity, but as viewed from the realities of what is observable in the early object relations of infants. We can then leave it open as to whether these considerations are of indirect relevance for psychoanalysis.

Stating the specific, non-epistemological, differences in the psychoanalytic and infant observational approaches

Let us first be clear about the specific objections to infant observation that are not essentially epistemological. Many psychoanalysts, André Green among them, have either criticized or dismissed infant observation for a number of specific reasons, three of which I address here:

1. Infant observation is forcibly concerned with action and interaction. Psychoanalysis, on the contrary, is concerned with mental "actions"—more specifically, with what happens in the psyche when action is prevented, delayed, or remembered. Both psychoanalytic theory and technique focus on the mental phenomena that result from the impossibility of specific actions directly reaching their aim. Infant researchers can only observe the actions.
2. Some psychoanalysts argue that almost everything of clinical interest is in the *après coup* ("deferred action", "*Nachträglichkeit*"). Some even claim that there is only the *après coup*. And strictly speaking, preverbal infants do not elaborate *après coups* of the sort that language speakers (thinkers) do. It is assumed that for adults all events are inserted into a vast symbolic network and take on their sense and psychoanalytic meaning when they have been processed and verbalized—that is, *after* the immediate experience. It is unavoidable in the talking therapies that most experience is recounted after the fact, since commenting on the immediately (passing) present instant is impossible. One is always running to reel in the disappearing past. But the preverbal infant cannot even do this. He does not have an extensive network into which an event falls, and in any case it is not symbolic and not explicable and amenable to the same psychic work nor to the same *post facto* constructing and telling. When one takes the position that raw experience is not simply reorganized *après coup*, but that form and sense is *created* after the fact, one is forced to conclude that the fragmented traces of passing raw experience have no organized form and sense in themselves, at the moment of their being experienced.

Accordingly, infants must live in a sort of experientially formless and senseless world of no interest to psychoanalysis.

André Green's point that there are no true *après coups* of the adult variety for babies is well taken. However, he goes on to conclude that accordingly there is nothing of psychoanalytic interest going on in the baby either. As we shall see he has gone too far.

3. André Green points out that infant observations mainly concern the baby in interaction with the object (i.e. in the presence of the object) but do not and cannot include exploring what happens in the baby's mind when it is alone, in the absence of the object, when the psychic processes of primary narcissism are in play—yet that is largely the subject of interest to psychoanalysis. In an important sense, psychoanalysis is a psychology of absence, while infant observation, focusing on the interaction, is a psychology of presence.

Addressing these differences in approach

Lived experience and the problem of "now"

Because action and interaction are what stand out as observable, and because there is no true, adult-like *après coup* in babies, what do we do, as infant observers? We necessarily become interested in the "*coup*". The *coup* is the raw experience-as-it-is-lived. It is the lived event that lays down the memory trace and somehow gets represented. But is that an issue relevant to psychoanalysis? It certainly was for Freud. But the lived raw experience has become a relatively neglected problem in psychoanalysis. The laying down of the memory trace is largely taken for granted, and psychoanalysts usually pass it over, except in the most cursory way—to get to the *après coup*. Developmentalists, on the other hand, are forced to address it. The lopsided interest of psychoanalysis in the *après coup* in comparison to the *coup* is curious when considering the central theoretical problems of translating experience into meaning, sequence into structure, and so on.

But what is the *coup*? It is a lived event that happens here and now. But when is "now", and where is "here"? I will start with the problem of "now". Immediately, we run into the problem of how time is conceptualized. Psychoanalysis has two main domains of time. There is the world time of physics (chronos), in which the present instant is a moving point that eats up the future and leaves the past in its wake. With this linear time, one can define the past and future, before and after, sequential order, and the temporal location of the *après coup*. However, the present instant, itself, is an almost infinitesimally thin, constantly moving slice of time, too thin for a whole event to happen in. The event must occupy a sequence of present instances as they move along. There is also in psychoanalysis a domain of timelessness, where chronos does not exist subjectively. This is thought to prevail in the id and in primary process thinking.

Such a conception of time is inadequate for describing lived experience. A present moment that has a duration is needed. And to conceptualize such a present moment one must turn to a phenomenological rather than physical notion of time, such as provided by several philosophers—Husserl (1964), in particular. In this notion, the present moment has duration in which a unitary event happens, such as a melodic phrase. This present moment is composed of three parts. The "now" of the moment when the "primordial impression" occurs; the immediate past of the "now", which is held active in a primary memory called "retention"; and an immediate future of the now, called "protention", which is a prefiguring or anticipation based on the consciousness of the retention. This present moment is bounded by a "past horizon" and a "future horizon". The movement from one horizon to the other is grasped as a single whole event with temporal duration.

Imagine that many of a baby's object-related experiences occur in and are structured during these Husserlian present moments. There are several features of such a view that are extremely interesting.

(1) First, what happens here and now is parsed in terms of present moments that have boundaries and an intrinsic form, otherwise they would not be perceived. The form is intrinsic in the sense of being coherent to the human mind and capable of being captured by our perceptual systems. A major problem in the parsing of on-line, raw experience is thus partially solved. The human

world, as it passes, is not a formless, senseless, unbroken continuum, with occasional innately salient events that stand out and can be built around. It is more a series of bounded, coherent, present moments.

I will purposely not call upon original phantasies, pre-conceptions, or *avant coups* to save the day and answer the question of parsing and giving form to experience, because they are too non-specific to answer it completely, and, if they can answer it only partially, the question must still get posed in its original form. So I return to the question: how could experience get structured in the very present moment of its being lived?

(2) Second, form is imposed by the mind on passing events as they happen, just as a melodic line is grasped *as* it is being heard, and is sensed as an entity. The assumption is that these contours, like musical phrases, are structured *as* they are being experienced, in the phenomenologically present moment. In listening to music, the form of a phrase is captured *while* it is being heard. It is not structured *après coup*, even though its perceived structure can be modified in the light of later musical phrases—that is, *après coup*. Still, it must get structured in the present moment. Its form is seized as it unfolds in time. As musicologists describe it, the musical form is revealed and captured by the listener as the crest of the immediate instant passes from the still-resonating past horizon of the present moment, towards the anticipated future horizon of the same present moment. It is interesting in this light to consider that the ability to predict the ending of a musical phrase that one has heard only the first part of is suggested to be universal, operating across different cultures—traditional Western and traditional Chinese, which have different tonal systems—and across different levels of musical education.

In other words, events occurring in the present moment are given an initial form as they are experienced and not only after, as during an *après coup*. It is important here to distinguish between two different functions of the *après coup*. One is simply to reorganize an already established form, sense, memory. That function is not at question here. The second function is *to create, for the very first time,* the form and sense, after the fact—that is, to take up the supposedly senseless and formless, fragmented impressions laid down at the moment of experience and provide them with a form or sense, later. It is this second, radical function of the *après coup* that I wish to question because it may not be necessary most of the time. If a form and sense are imposed during the experience, as I am suggesting, the *après coup* need not create, it will only revise, reorganize, and so forth.

(3) In fact, the revision process will start to occur during the present moment—that is, on line. Once again, music provides an excellent example. During the immediate future aspect of the present moment (the protention phase), a general anticipation is created by the trajectory of the retention phase. Imagine an unfinished series of notes making up a melodic phrase. The missing notes can generally be imagined. There is not an exact anticipation, but, rather, a family of implications, musical resolutions, that may be realized. And as any one particular implication is, in fact, realized, it revises the form and sense of what is still held in the retention phase. In other words, there is necessarily a primary revision during the lived present moment. I have gone into this detail to show that the young infant does not need a verbal symbolic process operating in the *après coup* to put into form, make some sense of, and even revise his immediate raw experience as it is happening.

(4) A further feature of the situation as described is that a present moment has what Husserl calls "longitudinal intentionality": it is heading somewhere. There is an inherent future or goal orientation. The infant, thus, is immediately immersed in a human world in which some of the basic underpinnings for a motivational perspective are present.

(5) What, then, are the forms that might appear for infants during present moments with their important objects? Imagine that the infant experiences its world in units of patterned flows of feeling that last split seconds or many seconds, or even minutes. I call these, "vitality contours". These vitality contours are made up of the instant-by-instant patterns of shifting intensity and hedonic tone over time, as occasioned by internal or external events. They are more like a musical phrase of feelings in flux which cannot be captured or even imagined by taking a single note—that is, a slice of time or a "sound-photograph", so to speak. Vitality contours are

global entities of feeling that are revealed only in time. They are analogic time contours that are best captured by dynamic kinetic terms, such as, "surging", "fading-away", "fleeting", "explosive", "tentative", "effortful", "accelerating", "decelerating", "climaxing", "bursting", "drawn out", and so on. They are like the trajectory of a desire as it travels to its immediate goal. And they occur and are processed in a phenomenologically present moment. These vitality contours do not reflect the categorical content of an experience, but, rather, the manner in which it is performed and the feeling that directs the action. It is for this reason that vitality contours underlie the appreciation of most abstract art forms that are formally devoid of "content", such as most music and much dance. Vitality contours are intrinsic to all experience in all modalities and domains. For example, a rush of anger or joy, a sudden flooding of light, an accelerating sequence of thoughts, a wave of feeling evoked by music, a surge of pain, a shot of narcotics—these can all feel like "rushes". They share a similar distribution of excitation/activation/hedonics over time, a similar feeling flow pattern—in other words, a similar "vitality contour". This account is an analogic, diachronic, micro-account of events as contoured and lived in real time. These are the events that make up the infant's relationship with its objects such as the phases of a feeding, a playing, a changing, and so on.

(6) This temporal format of temporally contoured feeling flows comprising present moments has the added advantage of responding in part to the problem of how preverbal infants represent experience. There is much reason to believe that young infants are precociously receptive to the temporal contour of events—sensations, perceptions, actions, affects. Accordingly, it seems most plausible that the vitality contour is a basic unit for the representing object-related experience.

Absence and presence

To any observer of infancy, it seems quite obvious that the events of greatest interest, intrapsychically as well as interpersonally, occur during interactions with the parents. It requires an elaborate rationale, inspired by a psychology of absence, to imagine otherwise—to imagine that what is of primary interest is what happens intrapsychically when the baby is alone in the absence of the mother. But since this is a widely held notion among certain psychoanalysts, it requires further examination.

Because of the nature of drives, the life of an infant is very repetitive, consisting of reappearing themes and variations to achieve the desired goals of baby and parent. It is in this context that the issue of the absence or presence of the object arises. André Green's suggestion (or criticism of infant observation) is that what is important for psychic work is the unobserved and unobservable infant in solitude, in the absence of the object. And, indeed, the psychoanalytic tradition has stressed the importance of absence in evoking phantasy, memory, and even thinking. I see it differently. What strikes me as most interesting and fruitful are the absences-in-the-presence-of.

What I mean is this. An event, a *coup*, can occur in the interaction, or when the baby is alone. During its happening, the experience is structured in the present moment, in the manner I have described above. When a similar event recurs, as it inevitably will, what evokes the infant's phantasies, memories, representations—in sum, his thinking—is the novelty of the second event relative to the first. It is the discrepancy between his already formed representation and the new happening that triggers his psychic functioning. One could call this a psychology of presence rather than of absence, but in fact it is a psychology of micro-absences, where it is not the absence of the object that is crucial but the absence of a match between the activated representation and what is happening now. The actual absence of the object is only an extreme case, and not necessarily the most interesting.

Adopting a psychology of micro-absences of match places the burden on the observation of interactive events that give clues to the nature of the infant's existing representations, its appreciation of discrepancy from what is expected or desired, its coping or defences to compromise, and the changes in its representations brought about by this encounter with a mismatch. This has permitted the creation of instructive methods such as the "still face" of Tronick and Cohn (1989) and Trevarthen (1987; Trevarthen & Hubley, 1978), or the "strange situation" of Ainsworth, Blehar,

Waters, and Wall (1978). It is why observation in-the-presence-of the object is necessary for inferring the representations of the object, or, as I prefer to say, representations of being-with the object.

Intersubjectivity

I will now bring intersubjectivity into our discussion of object-relatedness and representation. Intersubjectivity, after all, is crucial to thinking about infancy and psychoanalysis. The developmental starting point for intersubjectivity, however, is different in the two domains, and this results in different questions being posed. Before the baby can be intersubjective, psychoanalysis has required that there be a clear self–other differentiation—that is, not until the phase of primary narcissism is traversed. In a similar fashion, Piaget required that the infant be capable of "decentration" before he could appreciate or participate in an other's experience.

More recent views suggest that the baby, from the beginning, has two different, separate, and parallel perceptual and "participatory" systems. One is ego-centred, the one described by Freud and Piaget. The second is "alter-centred". This latter, other-centred system permits the infant to know implicitly and participate in the actions and affects of the other. The evidence for such a view includes the early imitation seen in young infants. Several hours after birth, they can imitate some facial gestures. When they can vocalize at several months, they can imitate short melodic phrases. These capacities require a perceptual engagement and participation that is centred in the other's experience. As the infant gets older and acquires new abilities, it will use them both in an ego-centred and an alter-centred manner, in parallel. In short, the preverbal infant develops from the beginning with an implicit knowledge of the other's experience that is not confused with his ego-centred experience, but is distinct from it and operates along side it. Such a revised view of the origins of intersubjectivity carries indirect implications for a psychoanalytic developmental metapsychology that are potentially considerable.

Finally, the infant's implicit knowledge of intersubjective phenomena has implications for understanding the processes of change which are relevant for psychotherapy as well as developmental change. Because infants are, by definition, without speech and do not use symbols, they have no access to explicit knowledge or symbolic networks in the strict sense, and they live in a world of an implicit knowledge of happenings. It is for this reason that preverbal-infant observers like myself have focused greatly on this implicit domain of knowledge, representation, and memory. That is what there is to work with. This same domain of implicit knowledge, however, is of great interest to all psychodynamic psychotherapies. A great deal of clinical phenomena of importance to psychoanalysis, including aspects of the transference, belongs to the domain of implicit knowledge. Christopher Bollas (1987) has referred to these phenomena as the "unthought known", and Joseph and Anne-Marie Sandler (1994) as the "past unconscious".

Let me be clear about the distinction between explicit and implicit knowledge. Explicit knowledge is verbal, symbolic, and declarative. It can be conscious or pre-conscious, but if it is unconscious it is generally under repression—that is, it is dynamically unconscious. Implicit knowledge, on the contrary, is non-verbal, non-symbolic, and generally resides in the descriptive unconscious. It is not under repression, but could be. It has never been rendered explicit. The intersubjective context between patient and analyst is largely implicitly known. And it is exactly this implicit intersubjective context or environment between therapist and patient that has become the subject of much focus in understanding the therapeutic change process. Shifts in explicit knowledge about self or the current intersubjective state are brought about mainly through interpretation. Shifts in implicit knowledge about the current intersubjective state are brought about through specific "moments of meeting" during which the two partners, in the course of improvising their dialogue, find themselves "being-with-each-other" in a different or new way that is an emergent property of their complex system of intersubjective relatedness. This is how non-linear, qualitative shifts occur. This is the essence of the change process, and it is as applicable to developmental leaps, big and small, as it is to changes in the analytic treatment situation. Once again, developmental processes and therapeutic processes have much in common.

Conclusion

I repeat, infancy researchers and psychoanalysts have much to tell one another, not to confirm or disconfirm notions within each domain, but to stimulate, inspire, and provide the wider knowledge base against which the concepts of each discourse will find their plausibility and general intellectual interest. Whether they listen to one another or not is another question. There is one final issue: "Who is a psychoanalyst?" Psychoanalysis is several things, and I am not referring to its many schools. It is a clinical endeavour with a theory and technique, it is a general psychology and metapsychological theory, and it is a developmental theory. André Green wishes to draw a fairly tight circle around who is a psychoanalyst and what is psychoanalysis. He argues that for contributions to the psychoanalytic notions of metapsychology or development to be truly psychoanalytic, they must arise in the clinical situation using the psychoanalytic technique. Indeed, *to do* clinical psychoanalysis, that is necessary. But is the clinical situation necessary *to think* about psychoanalysis, its metapsychology, and developmental theory? I would judge not.

In this sense, I do not accept André Green's basic tenets for this debate, namely, that he is speaking from within the walls of an embattled psychoanalysis, and I am speaking from without. For me, we are both within, but standing in different places.

CHAPTER SIX

Discussion (I)

Rosine Jozef Perelberg

It is a daunting task to formulate some comments on the work of two leading intellectual figures of our psychoanalytic time, by whom I feel I have, in different ways, been inspired. André Green is one of the most influential thinkers in contemporary psychoanalysis; our thoughts about "the observed infant" have been crystallized by Daniel Stern's work.

It is indeed staggering to think that Green's work has not until recently been widely translated into English. When I mentioned to a psychoanalyst attached to the Paris Psycho-Analytical Society that this debate between Green and Stern was taking place, I was surprised when he said that he did not know the work of Daniel Stern. It reminded me of how a visitor to our home after one of my husband's fieldwork trips to distant places asked us about the music we were playing. In response to our reply he asked: "Who is Mozart?" Within his own culture he was a cultivated man, but this event drew our attention once more to the fact that we can all be ethnocentric and treat our own culture as universal. Whilst the Jesuits attempted to convert the Indians in Brazil so that they could become real human beings, the Indians were drowning the Jesuits to verify whether they had souls. Humanity ceased at the borders of the tribe.

We are discussing here different psychoanalytic cultures, "different ways of thinking", as pointed out by Green. On the one hand, to quote some of Green's words in chapter one, he suggests that "no one single major discovery for psychoanalysis . . . has emerged from research". He adds: "There is a neglect in most of the investigations of the specificity of what is intrapsychic and unconscious, and an underestimation of the parameters of the analytic situation related to the concept of the setting." On the other hand, Stern suggests throughout his work that he has been able to chart some of the uncharted territory of infancy. Green, for his part, warns us in chapter four that it is important not to confuse the infantile (in all of us) and the infant. In his paper "L'enfant modèle" (1979), he points to the idea that observation studies hoped to find visible in the child what is invisible in the adult when the structure of the child has been derived from the knowledge of the structure in the adult. Green's thesis is that psychoanalysis is incompatible with observation. Observation cannot tell us anything about intrapsychic processes, which are the true characterization of subjective experience.

At the outset, Stern agrees that infant observations can never prove or disprove a clinical or theoretical tenet of psychoanalysis. Green would be in agreement with this. Stern proceeds to ask whether infant observation is indirectly relevant to psychoanalysis. He suggests that infant observations add to our commonsense knowledge about aspects of who a baby is. His aim is that of "imagining" the infant's subjective world (chapter five) and how he could represent its relational world. In another paper, Stern (1994) affirms that one cannot know the nature of the infant's subjective experience: we can only observe the interpersonal events that transpire between infant and mother.

In chapter five, Stern raises the question of how an experience can be structured during the very moment in which it is being lived. He brings the example of music, suggesting that "the infant experiences its world in units of patterned flows of feeling that last split seconds". Stern designates these as "vitality contours". "They are more like a musical phrase of feelings in flux which cannot be captured or even imagined by taking a single note" (p. 85). "For example, a rush of anger or joy, a sudden flooding of light, an accelerating sequence of thoughts ... these can all feel like 'rushes'" (p. 86).

The assumption is that, like musical phrases, these contours are structured as they are being experienced. In listening to music, the form of a phrase is captured while it is being heard. It is not, Stern suggests, structured *après coup*, even though its perceived structure can be modified in the light of later musical phrases.

The analogy with music, however, may lead us to another view. In his monumental series of volumes on the analysis of myths in South America, Lévi-Strauss (1971) suggests that "one cannot translate music into anything other than itself" (p. 646). There is a "radical impossibility of any transposition (of music) into an extrinsic language" (p. 646). In other words, the signifying function of music cannot be reduced to anything that might be expressed verbally. Lévi-Strauss further suggests that it is the audience that invests music with one or various virtual meanings, that it is the listener who is compelled to make up for the absent sense (p. 654). The listener attributes meaning to music in terms of his or her previous experiences.

Meaning is thus ultimately produced by interaction between the listener and the music. This analogy allows us to think that there is a meaning that is produced by the interaction between mother and baby which does not therefore relate to "what is going on in the baby's mind", which is, by definition, unknowable, or, to use Lévi-Strauss's analogy of music, irreducible to verbal understanding. This perspective is radically different from that which stresses the mother as the interpreter of her baby's behaviour. When the mother reinterprets the baby's feelings and thoughts, this is not an act of translation only but of formulation of meaning. This view points to the essential role of the mother's states of mind in the constitution of the child's sense of its own mind.

In discussing Stern's work, Green points to the confusion between the infantile (Freud would say that the unconscious is the infantile in us) and the infant. According to him, our true object, as psychoanalysts, is the infant in the adult, which has very little to do with the question: what really happened to the infant? The specific object of psychoanalysis is the unconscious.[2]

At this point, I would like to discuss two clinical examples. The first is connected with an ordinary piece of work that nevertheless indicates the multi-layered sources of analytic understanding. The second has, for me, more reverberations derived from observational studies.

"Anna"

> Anna comes in for the last session of the week. She is cheerful. After a period in her analysis when I could not say anything that felt right to her we have now been through a moderately good phase. She is happy with our work.
>
> She comes in and as she sits on the couch and takes her shoes off her ring catches on her tights and she says "shit". She then proceeds to lie on the couch and to tell me cheerfully about recent events in her life. Then she tells me of a dream. In the dream *she was dictating a letter to a secretary, Miss Clark, and tells her to have a slash. A colleague of hers (I will call him John) was watching this scene in a benevolent way.*

My patient has the association of slash with a violent tear. The secretary in the dream looked like her cleaning lady, who in reality has a name similar to mine. She had thought of firing her for ages before she left on her own accord. The associations to her colleague is that he is thoughtful and benevolent, but recently had commented that a mutual friend was going mad.

I myself was aware of the contrast between the cheerfulness and the "shit", which had come from "another scene" (the unconscious). John was also the name of a comedian she had told me about during a previous session. In one of his sketches, he was at a party and kept cheerfully saying "hello" to people, and "bastard" as he went away from them. Two levels of experience—the façade and the backstage, the conscious and the unconscious, the domains of reason and of the unreasonable, of madness. A binocular mode

[2] One would have to refer here to the entirety of Green's work, but I point specifically to those published in 1962, 1973, 1983, 1986c, 1993b.

of thinking, Bion might suggest. All these thoughts and associations led to the interpretation I formulated. Although my patient was pleased with our good work, there was a "shit", "bastard", coming from another (illegitimate/bastard) part of her mind, the very part that clamoured for our work to proceed and for the cleaning lady/analyst to be kept in her post. Concepts like projective identification, repression, censorship, and splitting might all come to mind now, which might account for that piece of work that related to an "unreasonable part of her mind", to use Peter Hobson's (1992) expression when he discussed Stern's 1992b paper at the British Psycho-Analytical Society.

Already in his 1915 paper "The Unconscious", Freud put forward his thesis that the unconscious is present in the gaps between the observable. The psychoanalytic domain is the domain of that which is, in fact, not accessible to observations but can only be reached through its derivatives. Thus it is easier to say what it is *not* than what it is: an absence of negation, of a sense of time, characterized by thing presentation, symbolism, and metaphor. The interpretation I formulated included my observation of the patient's behaviour, listening to her words, dream, associations, and impressions, including a familiarity with my patient's internal objects—past and present—and how all this reverberated in my mind at that moment. A piece of ordinary work which, nevertheless, indicates that the psychoanalytic domain is characterized by that which escapes us all the time, and which makes its presence felt through its absence. These "lapses", comments from "another scene", are a fundamental way in which the unconscious of the patient communicates with the unconscious of the analyst. The analyst's thoughts in a session, like the patient's, are not linear but are derived from many directions, which is what indeed allows us to reach a more "layered" formulation in our interpretations.

"Michael"

Michael is a young male patient who came to analysis after a serious suicide attempt that led to hospitalization. He was born blind and remained blind for the first two years of his life. A series of operations allowed him to gain sight. More than any other patient I have had in analysis, Michael made me conscious of the minute interactions between us in the consulting-room. The rhythm of our contact frequently evoked in me thoughts about synchronicity and timing in interactions between mother and baby. He was as aware of my minor bodily movements as I was of his, and I would often notice that in our bodily posture we were inclined towards each other. For instance, I would suddenly notice that if my head was slightly inclined downwards towards the left in a position of listening attentively whilst he was lying on the couch, he had his head tilted, also towards the left, in the direction of mine.

The right amount of contact was essential in our sessions: if I said too little, he would become quiet and withdrawn, almost lifeless; if I said too much, he felt too intruded upon and disorganized. The dance between us required a certain rhythm in which we should be intensely involved with each other. When I started to read the works of Stern (1977, 1985, 1994, 1995b), Trevarthen (1977), and Brazelton (Brazelton, Koslowski, & Main, 1974), I often thought of this patient. It was not that their work allowed me to understand him or what was going on in his mind, but that they evoked thoughts about a pace that should have been present in his interactions with his mother as a small child. What I have in mind is related to what Stern has discussed in terms of the ways in which mothers "tune in" to their babies. This was a relationship where mother and baby could not hold each other with their eyes and where bodily and sound contact appeared to me to have been intense.

However, other temporal dimensions were also present in Michael's material. In adolescence, his mind was filled with conscious fantasies of violence, and in young adulthood he engaged in violent relationships with his girlfriends and peers. Through violence he attempted to exercise his mastery over a world that was experienced as frightening and senseless. Some months into the analysis I began to realize that for Michael, in the transference, there was also an enormous confusion between intimacy and sexuality. He alternated between omnipotent phantasies of having seduced me into being his analyst on the one hand, and the terror of abandonment on the other. Different time dimensions could be comprehended in these experiences, the terrorized infant being cared for by a mother he could not see but feel and hear, the acquisition of vision and of language, and the advent of genital sexuality that was superimposed over that more primitive material. My suggestion is that these different time dimensions became condensed into one and externalized into patterns of relationships he established with his external objects. Essentially, I am talking about deferred action—that is, that different stages were relevant in the structuring of his phantasies (see also Sandler & Sandler, 1987).

Obviously I cannot go too deeply into what was a complex but rewarding treatment. My point here is that this example, to my mind, brings together contributions that I have been able to derive from the works of both Stern and Green. If some shapes and rhythms of a primitive mode of relating to the external object can be alluded to, meaning can only be derived *après coup*, after the emergence of symbolic representations and genital sexuality have retranslated earlier experiences.

* * *

The very few studies of outcome of babies observed in early infancy suggest that predictions do not seem to hold true except in a very broad way. This point comes across in the chapter written by Diem-Wille in the book edited by Sue Reid entitled *Developments in Infant Observation* (1997). In this chapter, the writer went back to children who had been observed as infants and compared the description of the child built up during the two-year observation with a follow-up observation two or three years after. Later life events had contributed to changes in the picture that the observer had built of the child.

Some important pieces of research are, however, available. The last twenty years have witnessed the publication of a number of studies of infant development. Works such as those of Brazelton (Brazelton et al., 1974), Trevarthen (1977), Stern (1985), Main, Kaplan, and Cassidy (1985), Hobson's work on autism (1993), and the studies by Fonagy and the Steeles (e.g. Fonagy, Steele, Steele, & Higgit, 1993) that focus on transgenerational patterns of attachment are among the most important. Fonagy and Miriam and Howard Steele have demonstrated that the parents' mentalizing ability (or reflective function) assessed before the birth of the child predicts the child's mentalizing capacity at 5 years of age (Fonagy et al., 1993).

Green reminds us that all this work does not have access to the complexity of the internal object and is prey to the uncertainty of knowledge. For Stern, it is behaviour that is at the centre of his researches.[3] Green asks how it is that one can move to processes of thinking from the procedures of experimentation. Maurice Godelier (1958), Canguilhem (1966), Joel D'Or (1988), and Widlöcher (1994) support the view that the essential difficulty arises when one pretends that empirical evidence is sufficient to establish enquiries about the process of thinking itself.[4] Canguilhem reminds us that behaviourism is not a science: it is a *philosophical position*.

In agreement with what Fonagy (1996) stated in his discussion of Wolff's 1996 paper, I think that what is so important in the kind of research that Stern is engaged in is "that formal observations of infant behaviour may set limits on psychoanalytic speculations regarding infantile experience by specifying competencies possessed by the child at various stages and ruling out as improbable genetic-developmental propositions that presume capacities outside the developmental timetable" (Fonagy, 1996, p. 406). Fonagy himself states, however, that the individual experience retrieved in therapy will have only a loose relationship to actual events of the past. Although the past may function like a dynamic template (to use the Sandlers' formulation, 1994), experiences, impressions, memories, and phantasies are reorganized by later experiences and may be revised at a later date, when the individual reaches a new stage of maturation (Laplanche & Pontalis, 1973, p. 111).

Edelson, a professor of psychiatry at Yale, has suggested that the great weakness of psychoanalysis has been its failure to provide its clinical findings with the necessary intellectual controls (cited in Robinson, 1993, p. 243). I would like to mention briefly a piece of research that has attempted to do just that. This is the Young Adults Research Scheme at the Anna Freud Centre, where sixteen patients have undergone analysis for the last eight years with analysts from the British Psycho-Analytical Society. What is perhaps crucial about this massive piece of research, whose clinical

---

[3] See Bratman (1988) for a discussion of the role of baby observation in the training of psychoanalysts.

[4] The whole of Volume 75 (1994, Part 5/6) of the *International Journal of Psycho-Analysis* is devoted to some of the current positions in this debate.

director is Anne-Marie Sandler, is the way in which the clinical assessments by the analysts themselves, carefully recorded after each session, are compared and contrasted with other more traditional evaluations. An experienced research psychiatrist administered a series of interviews prior to the beginning of analysis in order to establish current axis I (psychiatric illness) and axis II (personality disorder) diagnoses. A separate interview assessed whether the individual had an established borderline personality disorder. This is defined differently by Kernberg (1985), Gunderson (1984), and DSM-III-R (American Psychiatric Association, 1987) and information was collected to assess the three diagnoses (see Fonagy & Tallandini-Shallice, 1993). One piece of evidence that seems to be emerging from this mass of data is that none of the above assessments is predictive of a good outcome. The single factor that seems to be most correlated to good outcome at this point is the technique utilized by the analyst (for some clinical accounts of the analyses in this project, see Perelberg, 1999a, 1999b). Those analysts who concentrate their interpretations most consistently on the vicissitudes of the analytic setting itself seem to have a more positive outcome of their analyses. This seems to support a model of the individual in perpetual transformation in terms of *après coup*. The present is continuously reinterpreting and "transforming" the past. This view is essential to our analytic work.

CHAPTER SEVEN

Discussion (II)

Anne Alvarez

In this debate concerning the relevance of infant research to psychoanalytic theory and practice, I notice that both André Green and Daniel Stern have, at different points, raised the question of definition of terms, and I too wish to point out that some of the disagreements depend on the definition of research, others on the definition of psychoanalysis, and still others on the definition of relevance.

1. *The definition of research*: I shall follow Michael Rustin (1989) and other social scientists and philosophers of science in using a wide definition of research which includes not only the methods of experimental verification but also systematic qualitative research, naturalistic observational case studies, and the discoveries made in the clinical situation by the psychoanalyst.
2. *The definition of psychoanalysis*: André Green defines the subject of psychoanalysis as the unconscious, and prefers its paradigm to be that of the dream. I would point out that those of us who work analytically with children with thought disorder and cognitive deficits do have to become alert to problems of thinking

and of consciousness, and to paradigms other than that of the dream, such as play, movement, and temporal feeling shapes, and—at times—to a possibly even more radically different paradigm, that of development. Borderline, autistic, and many deprived children are different from borderline patients who are adults: for one thing, there is usually a much greater degree of developmental delay. One does find oneself having to get very interested in the problem of how a mind grows and, furthermore, in what might be the stages in the move from mental disorder to health and from, say, post-traumatic stress disorder (or chronic traumatic stress disorder) to recovery. Issues of the nature of, and steps towards, healthy development—however difficult and value-laden—do arise.

3. *The definition of relevance*: I agree that in one way nothing from outside is relevant to the moment in the session, but I believe that in another way anything and everything may be relevant. I recently read some words of Rilke's, quoted by two psychoanalysts, one writing a clinical paper (Symington, 1997) and another engaged in research (Bucci, 1997). Both quote it to illustrate the difference between superficial insight and deep insight. Symington is referring to the analyst's insight, not the patient's. The quotation is from Rilke's semi-autobiographical novel, *The Notebooks of Malte Laurids Brigge* (1958):

> I think I should begin to do some work, now that I am learning to see. . . . You ought to wait and gather sense and sweetness for a whole lifetime, and a long one if possible, and then, at the very end, you might perhaps be able to write ten good lines. . . . And it is not yet enough to have memories. You must be able to forget them when they are many, and you must have the immense patience to wait until they return. For the memories themselves are not very important. Only when they have changed into our very blood, into glance and gesture, and are nameless, no longer to be distinguished from ourselves—only then can it happen that in some very rare hour the first word of a poem arises in their midst and goes forth from them. [pp. 19–20]

Well, I love psychoanalysis *and* I also love infant observation and research, and I believe that *both* sets of findings—together with their theories and meta-theories—can become part of our blood in exactly the way Rilke describes. Lisa Miller, in the introduction to *Closely Observed Infants* (Miller et al., 1989), makes an analogy between the creative stance of the infant observer and the creative reading of a literary text. She points out that readers leave their knowledge of the writer and of his or her previous works lying at the back of their minds while they respond to the fresh immediacy of the impact of the new work. Symington (1997) says that we gain understanding from a "free-floating state of mind which has been primed by intense observation of the facts so that they become part of our blood. In this flowing state of mind we are not pushed or pulled to one side or the other but are open to the precipitation of meaning just as in a chemical solution in a certain optimal state a precipitate suddenly forms" (p. 276). And this is as true of infant research as it is of psychoanalysis, and I shall go on to say why. Below I give some examples of ways in which it has affected both theory and practice for me, and that will be my fourth point.

To return now briefly to the first point, that of the definition of research: Michael Rustin's writings on this issue (1989, 1997) are very helpful. André Green wants to protect the spirit of psychoanalysis from the invasion of the spirit snatchers, but another way of looking at the issue is that one aspect of the spirit of psychoanalysis *is* research. It leads to discovery rather than verification, to the generation of hypotheses rather than the testing of them. Rustin (1989) points out that the case study method is suitable for the identification of holistic coherence, and *recurrent, possibly hitherto unidentified, patterns,* and that psychoanalysis lies near one pole of the dichotomy of qualitative versus quantitative research, interpretative versus generalizing, intensive versus extensive methods, and both are complementary. He underlines (1997), as does André Green, the contributions made by great clinicians to psychoanalytic theory. I think he is right that infant observation is simply one step along the continuum and that we need the whole range. Neither pole need fear contamination by the other; indeed, they may be mutually enriching. I would add that neither pole need fear neglect by the other. If Colwyn Trevarthen (Trevarthen & Hubley, 1978) prefers to study only happy babies, Daniel Stern (1985) has not studied sexuality in babies, and Bruner (1968) studies cognition without including emotion, why should we mind? Take what seems to illuminate something for you, and forgive it for being only a partial truth.

A word, however, about the real number-crunchers. Most of the people who are studying interactional sequences are no longer measuring indices of total amounts of behaviour—they use techniques of sequential analysis which are very complex, and some of the models achieve something similar to the hypercomplexity and non-linearity experienced in the consulting-room. They take account of complex situations where, for example, the behaviour of an individual in an interactional sequence is dependent both on the immediate preceding response of the other and also on his or her own previous behaviour (Beebe, Lachmann, & Jaffe, 1997; Fogel, 1993; Schore, 1997). It can be an interesting exercise to translate their micro-analyses of intersubjectivity into a micro-analysis of intrasubjectivity—that is, to observe the relationships between thoughts through the lens of object relations, the dynamic relations between human figures (cf. Bion, 1962).

I will return to the subject of research, but first I want to say something about naturalistic infant observation. At the recent Second International Conference on Infant Observation held at the Tavistock Clinic, Lazar, Ropke, and Ermann presented an observation of a premature baby boy on an intensive care unit. Ropke described the baby's struggles, first simply to learn to be, as he struggled with basic processes like digestion and breathing, and then to begin to be able to manage a state of going-on being. She described the way that he seemed almost torn apart by huge twitches which shook his whole body during digestion and the constant struggle to get his breath and to exhale. She saw his whole body double up in obvious pain and shock. She also described the ruptures in his breathing, and the rare fleeting moments of peace when he could breathe easily. Then there came a day when she arrived to find him looking blissful and relaxed. She then saw him stretch forcefully as though he wanted to push something away and then pull up his feet and hands and turn his fists inward as if he were trying to gather himself together again. I have little experience with psychosomatic conditions, but I have seen many patients in states of fragmentation too great for projection to operate adequately, and the observer's delicate and finely tuned descriptions were for me a powerful and unforgettable experience. One really got a sense of what it could be like, at the very start of extrauterine life, not to be able to take even breathing for granted (see Lazar, Ropke, & Ermann, 1998). Rustin (1997) points out that sensitive observation and the use of the countertransference can make previously invisible material visible, just as Pasteur's microscope made the bacterium visible.

Turning now to the definition of the subject of psychoanalysis as the unconscious and sexuality: this is a big subject, but I would just like to say that it seems evident that the narrow two- or three-storey house (with excellent cellarage) of the topographical and structural theories has been enlarged by subsequent psychoanalytic theory-building. It now resembles something more like a spreading country house or Palladian villa where breadth and lateral thinking may offer as much to mental growth as that which lies below or behind.

Bion's (1962) theory of "alpha function", the function of the mind that makes thoughts thinkable, has been hugely enriched for me by Stern's (1985) concept of "vitality contours". Stern has, I believe, provided the "saturation" of Bion's unsaturated concept. Both thinkers have helped me to reconsider some of the preconditions and conditions for thoughts to become thinkable. The thoughts that I find myself working with much of the time with my psychotic, borderline, or traumatized child patients are not necessarily unconscious, and not precisely preconscious either; rather, they are thoughts that Bion (1962) called unthinkable and Bollas (1987) unthought—that is, not resisted or defended against but simply never dwelt upon or lingered over sufficiently either unconsciously or consciously. This is not implicit knowledge, because it is not known fully even unconsciously. Rather, it approximates to what Bion called a preconception. Some preconceptions have not even reached the stage of what the developmentalists call a pre- or proto-narrative or a pre- or proto-conversation. Clinicians trying to pick up very faint signals from an almost formless medium, and working to render such mini-thoughts thinkable, to turn preconceptions into conceptions, may need to study very early introjective processes at much greater depth than before.

I now wish to take the heat off Daniel Stern, and turn to Jerome Bruner, a cognitive psychologist uninfluenced by psychoanalysis.

In a classic work, Bruner (1968) studied the development in babies of something that he calls "two-tracked thinking", or the capacity to hold something in reserve, which he likens to the capacity to "think in parentheses". (It is fascinating to see this capacity develop in previously mindless psychotic and autistic children, and also in chronically depressed deprived children.) Bruner's speculations and research have been very helpful to me clinically in my work with autistic patients (but also with other, less ill patients, who nevertheless have some difficulties in using their intelligence fully). I had had the clinical experience of noting that certain of my patients could not think about the question "why", which involves being able to think about two thoughts at the same time. For example, I could not say to a patient in a state of psychotic fury and panic, "I think you are angry with me today because . . ." or "upset because . . ."—since at that moment he was so overwhelmed by anger and panic about disintegration that the "because" was an irrelevant luxury. I had also learned to my cost that, if a certain psychotic patient had recently managed to avoid falling into old perverse patterns, any attempt on my part to mention the past perversion could send him over the edge into it. Weak concentration needed strengthening, not weakening. That I knew, and other psychoanalytic clinicians, among them André Green (1986c, p. 309), have commented on this sort of technical problem.

Why do explanatory interpretations not work at certain moments? I had seen my patient close his eyes when he was trying to stay sane or in contact. But how fully to understand it, how to think about this, how to link it with other problems I was addressing, like seeing splitting as a development rather than as a defence in certain patients, was not at all clear to me. I was helped by Bruner's study (1968). Bruner observed babies developing from a newborn state of one-tracked attention, where they can either only suck or only look, to a coordinated capacity for two-trackedness at 4 months, where they can do both more or less at once. In the first days of life, they shut their eyes while sucking; then they begin to be able to *alternate* sucking with looking; at the third stage, they are able to "soft-pedal" the sucking, by engaging in non-nutritive sucking while they look at something. (One imagines that this something is likely to be the mother's face!) Bruner calls this third stage "place-holding" (pp. 18–24, 52), like putting your finger on a line on the page of a book while you speak to someone, which involves real coordination. Bruner has no interest in the psychoanalytic concept of splitting, but his study of the gradualness of the processes that lead to coordination may serve to remind us that there may be certain natural evolutions and necessary pre-stages or steps towards the overcoming of splitting and achievement of integration. It may also remind us not to rush them nor to try to skip any. (Note the difference between the psychoanalytic concept of integration and the developmental one of coordination: the former is a metaphor with spatial connotations—as are many concepts in psychoanalysis—while the latter is a temporal concept.)

> One adolescent girl appeared almost to have thought disorder as she tried to narrate the events of the day or her ideas on some subject. Finally, we learned that the problem was that, if she had four things to say, her mind would jump forward to the third and fourth, because she felt they were demanding her attention, and would not wait their turn in the queue after the first and second. Her own impatience and excitability were involved too, but her problem did connect for me with a possibly analogous situation seen in infant observation where the baby has the experience that, when it interests itself in something other than its mother, she can nevertheless wait attentively and interestedly in the background until it turns to her again. (See Alvarez & Furgiuele, 1997, on the need for both foreground and background objects in the development of two-tracked thinking.)

How do we get our thoughts to wait their turn, yet not disappear, and has it something to do with first being able to think at least one thought thoughtfully, and then, when we learn that there is space and time for two, to be able to think about two more or less at the same time? (See Alvarez, 1992, pp. 93–98, on other clinical implications.) I think that Bruner shed some light for me on issues concerning levels of splitting, modes of splitting, types of splitting, and steps towards, and conditions for, recovery from splitting. Some research findings—like, for that matter, works of literature and art, and the analyst's lived private experience—are irrelevant to our work, and others only confirm something we already knew. But the fact is that others do illuminate brilliantly something only half-known, and still others, I believe, do really teach us something brand new. I would hate to cut the otherness of the new (but, by the way, nowadays often friendly) scientific world out. It seems a bit like shutting the father out of the nursery.

CHAPTER EIGHT

Discussion (III)

Irma Brenman Pick

As a practising psychoanalyst of adults and a child analyst, I think of myself as a clinician, and I have also undertaken and taught infant observation along the lines developed by Esther Bick (1964). I am in broad agreement with the line of thinking that André Green has presented with great clarity. As he says, a considerable method and body of psychoanalytic research has evolved in the course of the twentieth century, which does indeed have a profound effect on our theoretical models and on our clinical work. These are neither pure theoretical studies nor single case studies, but the systematic investigation of a problem, using the specific and unique method of psychoanalysis. These studies, some of which are referred to by Green, have enabled our subject to develop in a lively way. For instance, Bion's (1962, 1963) studies of the theory of containment and the pathology of thinking, his work and that of Herbert Rosenfeld (1987) on projective identification and Rosenfeld's on destructive narcissism, Hanna Segal's (1957, 1978) on the pathology of symbolization, Winnicott's (1953, 1949) on "holding" and on, for example, hate in the countertransference, Betty Joseph's (1985) work on transference–countertransference, Joseph Sandler's (1976a) on actualization, to name but a few British analysts, have all had a profound influence on the theory and practice of psychoanalysis. From the so-called systematic studies, it is difficult to think of findings that have had a more significant impact on psychoanalytic thinking and practice. This is not a comfortable thing to say in a room filled mostly with those undertaking or having a special interest in Research with a capital R, Research defined as "scientific".

Furthermore, I do share Green's view that the overvaluation of "Research" often goes together with an undervaluation, or devaluation, of the research with which we engage in our psychoanalytic work. And if this Research (with a capital R) is privileged within psychoanalysis, we will, in order to placate and propitiate our enemies from without, succeed in destroying psychoanalysis from within. I believe this to be a "real" (not just a fantasized) danger! I was dismayed by the recent paper in the *International Journal of Psycho-Analysis* by Robert Emde and Peter Fonagy (1997), much though I may admire Fonagy's work in other ways. And I am concerned about the privileging of Research in the IPA, even if eventually we have to find ways to validate what we do and how we are doing it!

Having said that, I do believe that observation of and experience with infants and young children is an invaluable part of the equipment that a psychoanalyst might have in helping him or her to understand and empathize with patients' conscious and unconscious states of mind. Esther Bick (1964) pioneered the method of the weekly observation, in the natural environment of the home, of a young infant with its mother (and also father), a method now introduced into many psychoanalytic trainings throughout the world. These observations are informed by what we have learned in our psychoanalytic work about its meaning. Yet the observation itself also informs our work. Hence our "observation" is informed by our overarching understanding.

While these observations do not, to my mind, have the same status as those of the consulting-room, I do believe that the enhanced capacity to observe and experience something of the intensity of the relationship between infant and mother—and to experience whilst in analysis the intense feelings that this stirs up in the observer—is an invaluable introduction to clinical work. I have in mind experiences in the observer, ranging from rivalry and competition with either the mother or the baby, to all the wishes to intervene and interfere with the relationship being observed, which may stem from many different sources. These may include, for example, the difficulties of being left out of the intense intimacy of a joyful relationship, or conversely, reactions to what may be the almost unbearable pain of helplessly observing a maltreated infant.

It was Ferenczi who first drew attention to the importance of not only listening to the patient's words, but also attending to the pervading mood of the associations and observing the patients behaviour on the couch, including, for example, changes in the rhythm of breathing, other physical movements, and so forth. There is no doubt that the close observation of the infant sharpens the capacity to observe and monitor much that may be "beyond words". Moreover, these observations are neither contrived nor single observations, but there is, instead, the opportunity to follow whether, for example, patterns that may start very early are later repeated or are modified, and so on.

Let me use, to illustrate these points, André Green's most touching and telling example of the reactions of a 20-month-old child to her mother's "carriage" and miscarriages of pregnancy, and her relationship to her mother and to her mother's internal mother (the grandmother). The child, informed about a coming baby (after an earlier miscarriage), first looks for an infant who had previously been a visitor, then produces a doll and places it on her mother's belly, then disappears/withdraws into a cupboard, clings to a previously abandoned dummy, and later wants her mother to join her in the cupboard. For us, as I said earlier, the poignancy of this child's behaviour is informed by what we have learned in our psychoanalytic work about its meaning. Yet the observation itself also informs our work. For example: an adult patient (say, male), seeing another (new) patient for the first time or even meeting the idea that there could be a new patient, may become silent or miss a session/withdraw, or he may present a dream in which he seems to be withdrawn into a confined space/cupboard, or he may appear to cooperate but by his behaviour show that he is talking in a detached way or as if he produces the doll/baby himself, or sucks it all out of his own thumb, and so forth. Or he may try to pull the analyst into that "withdrawn" state with him; the analyst may find that she feels herself to be (psychologically) in a "dark space"—all observations with which we are quite familiar in the consulting-room.

We may all agree that the patient "withdraws", but this is not a robotic defence; he will have his unique way of withdrawing; the analyst will be concerned with understanding the gross as well as the more subtle nuances of pain and the many other feelings that are/were too difficult to bear. We may even agree that his reaction might be more appropriate to that of a small child than of the adult we see in the consulting-room. Nonetheless, to have access to that 20-month-old child's reaction brings a vividness to the understanding of the experience and of the pain of that "child-in-the-adult" in the consulting-room, which is not conveyed by using the words: "He defends himself by withdrawal."

A similar pattern emerges when we consider that the patient may "nudge" the analyst into joining him in the cupboard of that withdrawal from painful reality. That "nudging" may be thought or spoken of, by the analyst, in subtly pejorative terms, implying to the patient that if he, the patient, were an adult or a "proper" person he would be out there facing the problem—for example, of a new baby—without these difficulties. Yet if we think of the history of carriages and miscarriages in the life of that 20-month-old child, we might be better placed really to "understand" why the patient needs to withdraw and so on.

Furthermore, whilst I do not wish to "labour" the point (forgive the pun), and whilst I do not think of myself as a "developmentalist", I think that it is helpful to have an idea in one's mind of what age child (on the couch) one is dealing with at any moment; that is, who the "child" is, and to whom he is talking. That 20-month-old child's experience is different from that which one might expect in say, a 3-year-old. And, of course, the age of the child in the patient on the couch may vary rapidly from moment to moment—so the invitation to the cupboard may at one moment represent the avoidance of the intrusion of a new baby, and at the next may be sexualized, not only in the service of the oedipal struggle, but also as a defence against earlier pain. The earlier experience of intrusion may, for example, come from a breast, experienced—for whatever reason—as intrusive.

The experience of the 20-month-old is also different from that of a 3-month-old baby with a pregnant mother, where the confusion about who is the inner and who the outer baby may be even more perturbing. Or we may be dealing with a patient who psychically has more or less failed ever to leave that cupboard/womb in the first place. So again, whilst we may speak of neurotic or psychotic defences or states of mind, I find that I do have somewhere in my mind (and I find this helpful) some picture of the developmental stage of the "baby" on the couch, and of what it might mean to be that baby with that internal mother.

Similarly, in thinking about the internal mother of the patient, in the countertransference one may find oneself over-identified with the patient/child confronted with a new patient/baby, or, as a mother, overprotective about the new patient, fearing a miscarriage of the analysis. Whilst one may be required to address one's own issues, being able to relate to, for example, the plight of the mother with her history of miscarriages and her childhood history, is enriching to the work. These experiences, which begin with a careful monitoring of the analyst's own experience, may also link significantly with the history of the patient. Psychoanalytic thinking is currently much engaged with all these issues; my emphasis here is that the living experience of early infantile experience, primarily achieved through the reliving of this experience in the candidate's own analysis, is significantly enhanced by carefully thought through observation of the "real" infant.

And if this is true of infant observation, it is yet more true of the experience of working analytically with the young child and with the adolescent. Meeting with the intensity of the concrete experience of the passions of the young child (or the adolescent) provides an added dimension to understanding these experiences, or the defences against them, met with in the adult patient. Let me bring another example. Some 20 years ago I saw a video of Colwyn Trevarthen's study of very young (as I recall, 1-week-old) babies, timed for how long they focused on the mother's face and on the mother's voice, as well as on that of a stranger; the infant's focus was significantly longer on the mother's face and on the mother's voice than on that of the stranger. Then they presented the baby with the mother's face and simultaneously with the voice of the stranger. The baby went berserk, dramatically turning its head from side to side, showing considerable distress. Indeed, this was so painful to watch that it raises the question of the legitimacy of such experiments; what is going on, in the nature of the mother and the researcher, that permits them to expose the infant thus?

Many of us will have had the experience in the consulting-room of patients who believe that we speak with a forked tongue—for example, that we appear as though we were capable of caring whereas they "know" that we don't care and that we are just doing a professional job of work. For instance, I have a patient who is deeply cynical about my capacity to care, "knows" that I speak with forked tongue, and feels "safe" in this construction. He is, I believe, terrified of the underlying confusion and pain he would feel if he felt that I did care. This would raise, for him, unbearable issues about what is "true" and what is false in his object and in himself. I find that that picture of Trevarthen's baby stays with me with such a patient, although I understand that Trevarthen might well not agree with the use to which I put it!

I would also mention in this connection Lynne Murray's work with children of depressed mothers (Murray & Cooper, 1997), taking as her starting point Winnicott's views about the way that these children "mother" or ostensibly support their mothers or become disturbed in other ways. Her very innovative and sensitive ways of setting up situations that show so clearly the difficulties that arise confirm Winnicott's clinical findings and provide an enriched understanding; this promotes a fertile cross-fertilization.

And now to Daniel Stern. As he may recall from a discussion we had at the British Institute of Psychoanalysis some years ago, I am greatly interested in his rich observational findings, and we are indebted to him for the way in which he has validated, from a different angle, how important the first years of life are and the subtleties of the interactions between infants and their mothers or carers. I do think it is significant that researchers are able to show in experimental situations that infants do have a relationship with the breast/mother from the beginning of life. There is indeed an important meeting between the great intuitive leaps that Melanie Klein made some 60 years ago and the direct observations of infants that highlight the interpersonal (but, for Daniel Stern, not the intrapsychic) world of the infant from the outset. Yet I am always amazed and puzzled by the lack of acknowledgement for the theories that Melanie Klein, based on her clinical practice, was putting forward as early as the 1920s!

But I question Stern's implicit and explicit view that normal infants wish only to cooperate, to be attuned from the beginning. One of the cornerstones of Freud's discoveries is that we are not governed by rational behaviour only; it would be un-biological to think of the infant as only rational and adaptive to be later corrupted by its faulty environment. Furthermore, I do not quite understand why Stern shies away so much from any attempt to construct a picture of the infant's inner world whilst feeling free to formulate all sorts of other theories about that which he observes. I hope that he will forgive me if I repeat a question I put forward in our earlier discussion, and which for me remains unanswered. He tells us, for example, that the infant is an excellent reality-tester. This is surely partially true—any infant who, for a start, locates the breast and takes in nourishment from it must be a good judge of reality! But what happens to this perception after it has been affected by experience? Much research shows that traumatic experiences are relevant; whether due to external or other factors, perception is changed. The trauma and the way it is perceived and dealt with by repeated interaction between mother and infant forms a constellation, which becomes a perception stored and transferred to future objects.

In his work Daniel Stern quotes, for example, an experiment (by M. Gunther) that shows that a newborn whose breathing is accidentally occluded by the breast during a feed will be breast-shy for the next several feedings (Stern, 1985, p. 94). Powerful stuff this for infant and mother! Stern suggests that the infant clearly has memorial capacities, to register, recognize, and recall affective experiences, yet he (Stern) denies an inner world. Surely, in becoming breast-shy, the infant is now relating not to the "current" breast but to an earlier reality of a breast that threatened to suffocate. I suppose that behaviourists would say that he has been thus conditioned. I, following Melanie Klein, would say that he projects into the current experiential reality an earlier experience and is, indeed, so dominated by the memory of that earlier experience that he cannot relate to the current reality; perhaps this is the earliest manifestation of the transference phenomenon, and in line with Freud's concept of the transference. The perceptions, coloured as they are by the infant's own propensities, are stored and transferred to future objects. They then go through further transformations as a result of subsequent interactions. I illustrate this later with a brief clinical example.

Clearly, the infant is not able to perceive the event as accidental, nor could he write a PhD on the subject of it or his mother's intentions. I think that it is precisely because the infant's perceptions are not fully organized so that it cannot understand where it comes from that the occlusion may be experienced as so threatening. And if, in however momentary, unclear, tenuous, or murky a way, the infant imputes to its mother the intention to suffocate, why would it not also impute or muddle this with its own wish (and fear) to suffocate the mother with, for instance, its own demands for total and exclusive attention? In such ways I think that some of the observations that come out of empirical research are more interesting to analysts than Daniel Stern's theories allow for and, of course, correspond very well to our observations of patients who may, like Gunther's infant, turn away from analysis (*inter alia*) when they feel dominated by earlier experience. We are very familiar with the view that analysis fosters dependency, swallows the patient up, is suffocating, and so on; we are also familiar with the extent to which this theory may be muddled with or split off from any awareness of the patient's or critic's own determination to totally dominate and control the analyst.

I would also challenge the notion put forward by Daniel Stern that speaks of the validity of theories in terms of their common sense; I would remind him that Freud's theories of infantile sexuality outraged the "common sense" of the time, as did Melanie Klein's theories of early object relationships. And I am reminded here of Bion saying that one objective of psychoanalysis was to question why people failed to use common sense!

Significantly, however, many psychoanalysts who had earlier considered Klein's account of early object relations and of the paranoid–schizoid position and so forth to be far-fetched and implausible have felt enabled by way of the work of Daniel Stern (and, for example, Gunther and Trevarthen, discussed above) to reconsider her work. In fact, it turns out that, revolutionary though her findings were at the time, in some ways we may now consider that she was relatively conservative and cautious in her assessment of this very early relationship.

I do think, though, that we need to differentiate what may or may not be useful to us as psychoanalysts from what may be useful and really very valuable in the world of *real politik*! John Bowlby's work on attachment (1969, 1973, 1980) has been extremely important in humanizing the treatment of children in hospital. The value of it lies in preventing fractures in a relationship. But as psychoanalysts we want to go beyond fixation points to an understanding of what these mean in the inner world of the child and the interaction between the child's instinctual life and its experience. We know from our clinical work that the problem is not just a disruption in the relationship, but that deprivation stimulates murderous hatred. The child then does not know whether it is deprived or has, for example, caused the mother to disappear, or driven her away by virtue of its attacks. All this compounds guilt and the further need for grievance as a defence against such guilt and so on. This wealth of activity like hating and killing—for example, when deprivation is excessive—then complicates the experience of deprivation and negates positive experience. The whole awareness of separation producing yearning, loving, and hating becomes obliterated. These are the issues that psychoanalysts engage with, as André Green indicates, and these are the very issues that are not met in current empirical research.

Daniel Stern has written most fluently and interestingly, for example, on attunement between mother and infant—a very interesting area, of course, for analysts. But there seems to me to be scant space in his work for consideration of the inner world of the infant/child when this breaks down. I should like to illustrate how I would understand this with a brief account of a patient's dream. I am, of course, fully cognizant of the fact that this does not "prove" anything!

> A young male patient (the son of a mother who was depressed in his infancy) falls passionately in love, early in the analysis, with a young woman, S. He arrives for his analytic session telling me that although he spoke to S on Sunday, he then

became very distressed when he failed to reach her on the telephone yesterday. He felt desolated and devastated. He could not understand it—it felt quite out of proportion. He went on to say that it all has an archaic feel about it. He then told me the following dreams (I shall present a condensed version of the dreams and of what took place in the session).

1. He dreams that *he is in the roof/girders of a very old building—scrabbling around in there—like an animal or a rat.*
2. *He is driving—two roads are coming towards each other—they don't meet. One is higher than the other; somehow where they should come together they do so in a way that is quite blurred.*
3. *There is something about the name "Sophie".* He associates this name to one shared by his girlfriend, his mother, and his sister—and the Queen of his country of origin.
4. *He meets Prince Charles—but addresses him by a more or less intimate, less formal name.*

He brings many associations to these dreams. These and the dreams themselves, and my former knowledge of this patient, lead me to interpret that the desolate, devastated feeling that he described at the beginning of the session, linked with not "meeting" S on the phone, was represented by the two roads that don't meet. He did not experience this as a failure to meet, but filled this in, not with ordinary disappointment but, albeit in a blurred way, with his theory. I suggested that when he wished to meet S, this came with a princely command. I thought this applied to the present wish to "meet" with S, but was also associated to his mother (and sister) and to the Queen. (I felt that he was too upset for me to say that if he was not the Royal Prince, he felt himself to be a right Charley!)

I also considered and interpreted that when the meeting does not happen he feels angry and hateful, and he deals with this by scrabbling around in a rat-like way, as he believes in the rafters of S's mind and "establishes" a theory that she is not there because she feels angry and hateful and takes a superior position in relation to him. This, I suggested, is the blurred meeting of the roads—that is, where he is not clear whether the hatefulness comes from S or from himself. He surprised me by

> bursting into noisy tears, like an infant, and when he recovered he said that he felt quite overwhelmingly relieved. I was then able to link all this with my not being available to meet him over the past weekend and in the coming holidays, and the very painful conjunction of this together with his feeling rejected by S.

I hope that this small piece of material may serve to illustrate the processes that, in however blurred a form, an analyst would think of as going on in the internal world.

Hate and the wish to kill and the projection of that hate are as much a part of the infant's propensities as its capacity to love and its projection of that love. And these features colour its perceptions of and its reactions to events in the external world, just as these external events have their effect on its inner world. There is always an interaction, and this is not just an issue in the interpersonal relationship but essentially in the intrapsychic world.

I should add that some days later, following a more tangible rejection by S, this patient—who has respiratory problems—dreamed that *there was a cobra wound around his neck, and he was desperately holding on to its head to stop it from spitting and biting*! My view would be that these feelings, in the present and in the relationship with the analyst, have archaic origins, which go right back to the time of spitting and biting, and which of course go to colour and form the internal world of the child. It is this domain that for me is central and is missing from the world of Research.

Nonetheless, the work of Daniel Stern and others is, and will continue to be, immensely useful in alerting the world to the crucial importance of the early infant–mother relationship. The "powers that be" need to be persuaded by that kind of Research, and it plays an extremely important social and educational role, which is to be applauded. It may, in the real world of today, also be that "outcome" studies are needed for funding, but I think that it is of the utmost importance that they do not begin to dominate our thinking as psychoanalysts. The current desperate rush to survive by achieving "respectability" may, in fact, jeopardize the very specific and very powerful capacity for research that psychoanalysis has in fact demonstrated and it continues to embody.

CHAPTER NINE

Plenary discussion

André Green

The interesting remarks the discussants made would, of course, need detailed answers, but we must limit ourselves here. I will essentially try to answer Anne Alvarez' remarks, because I think that she is the only one who had a different view about what I had to say. She discussed my idea of the dream as a paradigm, and she brought our attention to some patients in which dreams would not be the paradigm. Well, the problem is, dream is the paradigm for psychoanalysis, and for the psychoanalytic conception of the mind. That there are other conceptions of the mind is not questionable; but if we think it over, we see that what is important in the dream, as Freud analyses it, is the unconscious fantasy during the previous day.

And I would ask about the other patients whom Anne Alvarez mentions: isn't she interested in the unconscious fantasies of these patients? Now, it is true that one has to pay attention to thinking,

---

Editorial note: This chapter contains edited extracts of the plenary discussion.

to play, to movement: thinking as Bion described; playing as Winnicott; movement as Freud. So I do not see any point here, because what Anne Alvarez is doing is only a shift of emphasis. The idea that the unconscious is linked to an invisible activity still holds.

Again, I think that Anne Alvarez offered me the same objections as my objection to Daniel Stern. Now, we hear of babies who "learn to be". What does that mean? Is this not metaphorical—that is, very expressive, very evocative? I'm sorry, but it is not a scientific hypothesis. Learning to be, or fighting to be—I do not say that is something that is self-explanatory.

Now, about the idea of natural thinking, and the idea that the "why" has to be replaced by the "what"—here, I must make a very important hypothesis (which I am sure will raise a lot of disagreements). That is exactly what Freud said about the id. And this is the main difference between the unconscious and the id: in the id it is not a question of why, it is more the question of what; however, this needs further explanation, but I cannot enter into detail here.

I agree with 95 percent of what Irma Brenman Pick said—I have saved five percent just for the sake of discussion. My discussion concerns the way that she has tried to combine my perspective with Daniel Stern's about the experience of the "now", but this too, I think, will come up in general discussion. To emphasize the "now" is also, I think, to bypass the specificity of the unconscious. The "now" is very important for the registration of conscious experiences, and what is important is what the mind is going to do with that "now", how it is going to transform it, how it is going to attribute it to the self; and this implies deformation. You cannot get away without it.

Now, to end with, and to say a word on Rosine Perelberg's comments—with which I also agree in parts—my agreement with her is biased because she can read French and so, since only ten percent of my work has been translated, she knows better than many others what I am talking about. Rosine Perelberg was right on a very important point, and I think that this is the real issue, which we need to discuss further at length here: we are dealing not only with a theoretical problem—we are dealing with cultural differences. Cultural differences between the Europeans and the

Americans, and, within the Europeans, between the French and the English. And all sorts of major reference works which are different in the different places, and this is an explanation of the state of fragmentation of psychoanalysis. And if I may add one remark: when the patient says, "Hello, bastard", what she is showing is that this has to do with the illegitimate child born out of a prohibited sexual relationship. This is the meaning of the word "bastard". But what it becomes is that these thoughts became bastardized in her mind. These are illegitimate thoughts which have the status of being bastards, which means that they have to be put aside, discriminated, prohibited. This is not only a matter of hiding and showing, it is also about infantile sexuality and fantasies. And when the patient seems to mix up sexuality and intimacy, this is also the same process. Intimate thoughts—bastard. Sexualized intimate thoughts—bastard. Intimacy here relates to the inner self and the sexualization of inner states of intimacy which can also be a defence. I have to stop there—I will have many other things to say, in particular to Daniel Stern.

JOSEPH SANDLER

I am going to take the liberty of intervening with a suggestion about the use of the term "the unconscious". André Green knows so much more about Freud's writings than I do, but nevertheless I will take the liberty of making these comments. In the topographical model of the mind, the unconscious—the dynamic unconscious—referred to what had been repressed, what lay behind the infantile amnesia, and so on. And then the term "the unconscious" was used—and Freud was quite explicit on the point in a descriptive sense—to include the preconscious. But there is an enormous difference in the functioning of the dynamic unconscious and the preconscious. And what happened then, in 1923 and thereafter, was that when Freud had the structural theory of superego, id, and ego, he referred to the whole part of the mind that was unconscious, including the unconscious ego, as "the unconscious". A terrible confusion. Now that confusion has persisted in the discussion here, and I think that it is very important for us to keep in mind the distinction between, let us say, the early infantile fantasies (e.g. primal scene fantasies, etc.)—about which we will hear something, I am sure—and the current thoughts that the patient has in the present (e.g. transference thoughts) that are, descriptively speaking, unconscious. In the topographical model, they would have been preconscious; they are in the unconscious ego of the structural theory, the second topography; there is a difference between these various terms, and they are significant. That is what I wanted to stress. And so if we talk about the unconscious, I think we should delineate what we are referring to a little more precisely. It would help us, and I think it is relevant to the issues that are coming up, because a great deal of research that is being done has to do with what Daniel Stern referred to as implicit knowledge and so forth, which we would attribute to the dynamic unconscious in the topographical theory, also to aspects of the unconscious ego of the structural model.

DANIEL STERN

Let me briefly make just a few points; hopefully, we will get to them in more depth later. One thing I want to say that I did not say earlier, and which is important to me, is that I have an enormous appreciation for André Green's work. It has meant a lot to me, and I have learned a lot from it. I think that one of the differences between us is that I see him as really being a psychoanalytic purist in important ways—I will not say minimalist, because that would be too constraining—whereas I see myself as much more interested in bridging, much in the way that Anne Alvarez talked about; I am keenly interested in different disciplines and seeing what happens at the interface between them. And I make this distinction between us because I think it helps clarify some of the disagreements or potential disagreements. For instance, this business about references—André Green mentioned that I cite only a few psychoanalytic writers. Well, if I am writing an article, such the one in the *Infant Mental Health Journal* (Stern, 1994), I know who the readers are, and I know what language they will accept. And so when I talk about motivation sometimes instead of drive, and I use only the really necessary references to psychoanalysis, it is because I know the audience for whom I am writing. Now sometimes, because I am interested in this interdisciplinarity, I feel a little bit like—well, to say a "whore" is a little too exaggerated—

compared to the purity of the position that André Green can maintain; I respect this position, but it is not the way I see the world, so I have to act differently. And I think that this is a very important difference of how one proceeds. So my feeling is that the important point about the references that were in the *Infant Mental Health Journal* is that several thousand developmental psychologists in America and some in England are now going to read André Green's work for the first time. That is what I see as the important bridging function that happens when you do have the effect of indirect relevance, as I have been talking about, from one field to another.

With regard to Research, with a capital R—or with any kind of R for that matter—I want to pick up on a point that both André Green and Irma Brenman Pick made. In some respects, I agree with them very much that research can be very dangerous for psychoanalysis if Research, with a capital R, is let inside the corral and starts to dominate it. But one of the reasons is that research is dangerous for any set of thought because most of it is terrible. The problem is really with the pressures, the quality of research that gets produced is often not very good. From the point of view of what really would help, I would believe in a policy more of having the government pay researchers not to publish, rather than the other way around. So part of it has to have been extraordinarily selective with referring to what is the nature of the research that would be allowed to, so to speak, function in it, and of course there are real problems with that.

There is one area that has come up a couple of times now where I do not agree. I more or less insist on the fact that I am studying what I will call the inner subjective world of relatedness with the object. It may not be a psychoanalytic way of doing it, but you cannot say that I am not interested in the inner world or in the inner world as it concerns relatedness, since that is really where the whole thing is directed. To say that it is not the traditional analytic way, or the frame of mind with the methodology that analysis uses to do it, is another issue. But I do not accept that this is just behavioural and external and on the surface. If you only have behaviour, which is all you can observe, and that is your main method, then that is what you infer from. It does not mean you are stuck there, and it does not mean that you are a behaviourist. And I think this is an important point.

This gets back to the same problem with the "now". As André Green mentioned it, I agree that the "now" is of greatest interest to psychoanalysis, to the extent that whatever happened then becomes meaningful and inserted into a lot of other structures and integrated with them. But my question would be this: who, in fact, is going to give psychoanalysts an idea of what is the "now"? And I am saying that it is the people interested in infant observation who have been led to question the "now" more. Because you can say that what is interesting is what the mind does with the "now". At some point you have to know what happened at the "now" too, because there is not only the *après coup*. So I see these as complementary, and you cannot dismiss it by saying that the other thing is the more important.

One thing about music, a topic Rosine Perelberg raised—I think that my issue is, perhaps, more with Lévi-Strauss than with her. I agree that music cannot be translated into anything else than itself. Where I disagree is that music would not exist, would not have been invented universally, if it did not correspond in some very important way to the manner in which the human mind parses its own experience. And philosophers have always made the point that, in fact, music is the only medium that one has in which emotions in the abstract can be experienced, disconnected from the contingencies of real life, which is an extraordinary thing. And since the baby does not have a lot of other ways to translate it, and the baby is put into a situation where most of the world, at least in the beginning, consists of abstract music and abstract dance, the question is, how will that get parsed? How is the baby going to go about identifying meaningful structures as they get lived, since it cannot do much with them afterwards, when it is put into this sound-and-light show and movement show? And that is why the issue of movement is too easily dismissed, or of dance, if you say, "well, you can't translate it into anything else"—I am not worried about that. I am worried about realizing that music in fact, for me, is no different from human behaviour for the baby. As I say, it is like a dance or music: that it is the only thing that there is going to be for a period of time.

With regard to the issue that Irma Brenman Pick brought up about the missing of the pathological in my work: my feeling is that I have to agree with her in part. Let me say that there are some sort of strategic reasons for that. One of them is that it is a necessary starting point for most infant observation not to borrow a psychopathological model in which to understand things. So the tendency is not the clinical one of seeing things in terms of pathology—that's an important overview. Another thing is that it is not really that the babies I see in Geneva or New York are different to those in London. What I consider from my perspective to be aggression and destructiveness on the part of the mother, or of the baby towards the mother, from a Kleinian perspective looks very different. This is because the units of experience that I am talking about are much smaller, because that is where I think the baby is living. So that I see aggressiveness, for instance, occurring in the smallest of acts all the time; I have never seen a good mother–infant relationship where there is not something almost at the edge of disaster occurring every nineteen seconds in the course of the interaction. But at this stage of development I have not tried to push that towards a pathological model, and I do not know if I ever will. I agree that this may represent a lack, but it is not a lack in the method or in the approach: it is simply not where I have taken it up to this point.

André Green

Daniel Stern said he disagreed with some of the things I said about his work. But if you take, for instance, the problem of basic assumption, this is what I have been discussing all the time. I do not deny at all that there are other conceptions of the mind, and that there are very valuable thinkers outside psychoanalysis who can teach us something about the baby, the mind, and everything else. What I am really concerned about is the specificity of psychoanalysis, and I question whether Daniel Stern's work can be of relevance, whether direct or indirect. There is a matter for debate—it is the question of movement. This is a very personal interpretation of Freud, but I have to give it because I think that it clarifies what we are discussing. I was in agreement with everything that Joseph Sandler said about the first topographical model.

In my opinion, what Freud brought with the so-called structural model—the Americans have baptized it this way—is that when it is not only the question of the unconscious ego, about which, of course, Sandler is right, it is the question that there is a change of emphasis, if not of paradigm. If you read in the *Introductory Lectures* (1933a) Freud's comments on the id, there is not any mention about representations. On the other hand, what we would call in the ego a representation, in the id Freud called an instinctual impulse. So the reference to movement, internal movement, is here of primary importance in Freud's work. The drive theory is a theory about the dynamic point of view, mainly in terms of movement. Even before "representation". This is my first point.

The second point is about behaviour. Daniel Stern objects that it is he who has written about behaviour; I have quoted him from his book *The Interpersonal World of the Infant*. He describes the basis of the relationship with the Other. He says that it is not the behaviour of the person perceived, but, I quote, "rather some aspect of the behaviour that reflects the person's feeling state". Daniel Stern is obviously embarrassed because he wants to make the distinction between symbols, signs, and what he is trying to describe as feelings. And, of course, there are not many people who have dealt with this question. Charles Sanders Pierce did. So we cannot rely on some existing body of theory, because when he speaks of a vitality contour, I agree with vitality, but I cannot see how vitality—a thing that he describes as unlimited, undefined, spreading all over—can have contours. Contour is related to form; affect is not form. Language is form, representations are forms, but affects are not forms. So the question of the behaviour is not me accusing Daniel Stern, these are his own words.

And, to end with, about music. In my book on affect (1999a), the epigraph is a verse that you all know by heart, because it belongs to your culture more than mine: "If music be the food of love, play on." So the question of affect is of crucial importance, and I do not think that affects are the basis of everything. I think that representation is as important as affect, but that the mind is divided in these two activities, which are in conflict and to some extent contradict themselves. And about the mixture of psychoanalytic knowledge with external knowledge: I am reminded of the French joke about the skylark paté (see chapter four), made from a skylark—and a horse. This mixture of skylark and horse is what I have noted about lists of references. One skylark—the psychoanalytic references—and a horse—all the other references. And Daniel Stern cannot deny that many of the authors on whom he relies not only do not consider psychoanalysis, they fight it. I will not commit suicide.

NICOLA DIAMOND

I want to make a comment on the question of temporality and moment, and deferred action or *après coup*. I think that there is some misunderstanding here. I would just like to add a little bit to say that temporality is a process. It is the way time is always already in movement—that the present is never pure present, it always relates to the past and it always relates to the future and it is in motion. So I think that when Daniel Stern is talking about moment, he is also talking about a deferral process, even in that smaller moment, because in that—well, I am actually in between—I am actually suggesting that *après coup* does not just happen when we are adults, and it does not just happen when we have linguistic acquisition. Language is a much more complex process. It is very much the preverbal, which is the exchange of meaning in a communication, in an interaction, in a relationship, where public language—which is not only linguistic—emerges. Now, language is the way we make significance and meaning, but that can be understood in a much broader sense. And I think that when we are looking at the infant and deferred action as process in the infant, we are looking at meaning in the making, significance in the making. We are looking at the difficulty of making meaning and significance in a relationship. But we are looking at temporality of process. Otherwise, we are kind of mapping onto temporality only a notion of pure present moment, which I think could be misleading. I feel that my point is really an addition, not a criticism.

SHEILA SPENSLEY

I was thinking about the controversy of knowledge and how we gain knowledge, and whether it is by the methods of empirical research or of psychoanalysis. And I wondered whether one of the difficulties that emerges is due, perhaps, to not differentiating sufficiently what we mean by knowledge, and how we come by it.

That is to say, I think we can have implicit and explicit awareness or experience. We can observe, and that is a kind of experience too. But something else has to be added to make it knowledge.

John Southgate

My question is for André Green. (It is very good to meet a French analyst, because all my knowledge came from Lacan—who was hardly unprejudiced.) Because I know that Daniel Stern knows the psychoanalyst John Bowlby really well, and Bowlby is a psychoanalyst in this country whom we—or at least some of us—take very seriously, what I would like to ask is: is it cultural, is this one of the people whom French analysts would read, would know, and, if so, would you consider him to be a psychoanalyst according to your own definition? I should add that, as you know, Bowlby used all the contemporary sciences, from evolution to you whatever you care to name.

André Green

To take up the first point, I think that it was the right way to put the problem under the heading of temporality. I have been working these last years on the concept of time in psychoanalysis. This is, in Freud's words, a very complex one. It is so complex that in the history of psychoanalysis, as it proved too complicated, the psychoanalysts had only developed one aspect of it, which became known as the developmental perspective. After this, all the other aspects, which are sometimes self-contradictory in Freud, have been forgotten or undervalued. Let me name just a few aspects that I can remember immediately (when I go back home, I will probably find two or three others). There is first the *après coup*, which Freud developed in his Project (1950 [1895]); you find the most important information about it there. Then you have the *Three Essays* (Freud, 1905d), which bring the developmental point of view. But if you think of what Freud says there, he gives the lava-flow metaphor: when you reach one stage, the preceding stages are still already there—there are flows of lava. So one cannot speak of a moment, dissociating it from the preceding ones; it is all going on in kinds of different waves mixing up. Third, we have the notion that the unconscious ignores time. Fourth we have the idea of the persistence of the sexual theories of children. Fifth, we have the repetition compulsion, which is something different that formed the idea that the unconscious ignores time. Sixth, you have the notion of the primal fantasies, with which Daniel Stern said he would not agree. Then, seventh, historical truth—a concept completely forgotten in psychoanalysis. So you have at least seven self-contradictory aspects of time.

So what are we going to do with the "now"? There is evidently a basic misunderstanding. I do not hope to convince Daniel Stern here—it is not in a discussion like this that I will succeed. It is by developing it in my writings that I hope I may perhaps have an influence on what he says. But the person who spoke of temporality brought up the question of meaning. Meaning is a very general concept. What we are interested in are the forms of unconscious meaning, and the specificity of the unconscious meaning—in other words, the relationship of meaning to different types of representations, including representation as the psychic representative of the drives. And, in repetition compulsion, what Freud speaks about as a kind of amnesic memory.

Now, the question about John Bowlby. This is a very pertinent question, because I believe it was Bowlby who first brought the scientific spirit into psychoanalysis. He gave an interview—I think in the *Free Associations Review*—in which he said about Anna Freud and the others: "Those people had no scientific mind. They did not know what science was." Now again, I raise the question: has psychoanalysis to be related to science? This, of course, will raise a huge protest, but I think that the question deserves to be posed. So, I believe that John Bowlby's ideas have probably influenced many people. But I also think that his views of attachment theory are totally irrelevant. For instance, I do not see in any way why attachment theory would run against drive theory. To me, they are two aspects of the same thing. But, in the end, you must have options, and going back to one of my favourite writers, Winnicott, I re-read the following—it is from his paper on the true and false self, written thirty-seven years ago: "My experiences have led me to recognize that dependent or deeply regressed patients can teach the analyst more about early infancy than can be learned from direct observation of infants, and more than can be learned from contact with mothers . . . with infants" (1960, p. 141). I could stop here and say—see, I have Winnicott on my side. But I will be honest and read how he continues: "At the same time, clinical contact with the normal and abnormal experiences of the infant–mother relationship influences the analyst's analytic theory, since what happens (in the transference in the regressed phases of certain of his patients) is a form of infant–mother relationship" (p. 141). This is not French psychoanalysis: this is your patrimony.

Daniel Stern

There are two main points I would like to make about the issue of temporality. One is that I think that it is going a little too far to say that within the "now", the present moment, there is already a built-in *après coup* or a deferred action or whatever you want to call it in this case. The reason I say that is that, conceptually, you have to decide where your units are, and what are the boundaries of the units. And if you want to place the boundaries around a chunk of time in order to have something like an entity that is global, then you have to make a distinction. Now I agree in a philosophical sense that it is almost arbitrary, but I cannot truly argue with André Green's position except to say it would not be very heuristic to do it that way, it would not get you anywhere. I see this problem almost like the problem of light: is it a particle or a wave? It's both. So I can see the *après coup* as acting both within and beyond, but, more importantly, I think that it is easier to conceptualize the world—especially the world that the baby has to make up—if you treat it as what I will call a wave, in that you need to have a whole unit. I certainly agree with you that there are *après coups* before language, because in fact the same thing gets re-presented with variations, or with non-variations, or with slight variations.

Two things with regard to temporality—and here I open this up as a point of discussion with André Green and the rest of you—is that in the seven aspects of temporality that André Green mentioned—all of which I agree are distinctive and very important—from my perspective lack two things. One is they do not talk about time as an analogue function—in other words, something that has an analogic form, like a curve. They talk about it as a digital event, whether it is sequencing or synchronicity. This is very important, because my whole notion of a contour has to do with time as an analogic experience, just as a melody is an analogic experience compared to notes, which are digital. This is a very essential distinction. Another thing is that in all of the kinds of time that André Green mentioned, there is no diachronic account of what happens within an event, only in comparison with another event. And if you are going to take an analogic view of the flow of time, and try to get inside it, that gives you an entirely different picture of the world of time. And that is what I am arguing for, that I feel is different. And that leads me to a third thing that I think will probably have to be discussed over a long period of time, because I am not sure quite how I feel about it. But my intuition is that I do not agree with André Green when he says that affect has no form. I think that he says that by virtue of the fact of some of the theoretical positions that he holds. I would say that affect does, in fact, have a form, and the secret to the form is its analogic time-form. That is the subjective experience of affect, even though you can slice it like a photograph, into certain representational functions or certain memorial functions. But effectively it has a form, and that is part of what I am suggesting or throwing out as a hypothesis, not a fact. Sit with it and see how it feels. And I think we can discuss that further.

Mauro Morra

Although I found the discussions and the presentations quite important and interesting, I must express a bit of uneasiness. The controversy seemed to me more about the methodology than the conclusion. If it were a comparison, and even a controversy, between or among the different conclusions, of course it would be more relevant, in my opinion. I think that there are different ways of observing this. Certainly the position of the psychoanalyst is a particular one. There are also observations, the direct observation of the infant, and I think that each approach can bring something important, provided that it is clear what the differences are. First of all, I would say that in London, in both the British Psycho-Analytical Society and the Tavistock Clinic, infant observation has a particular meaning, which means the observation of the baby, the infant, according to the Esther Bick method, and it seems that your observation is quite different from the methodological point of view. And I think that this is important too, because, of course, the observer is a presence: a presence with whom the parent reacts and often the baby himself or herself reacts. We know there is a lot of work about it. Certainly if you compare infant observation with the psychoanalytic approach, there is also another really important difference. And that is that, in a psychoanalytic approach, our understanding is in some way getting an immediate response from the patient. As Freud said, not every "no" from the patient really means "no". Anyway, it is an immediate answer. When we observe the baby or the infant, we have no immediate response to our speculation, I could say.

Nicola Diamond

I actually wanted to say something about André Green's presentation, because I found it quite inspiring. As someone who teaches and supervises counsellors, I am in a rather different area of work from some of you here. I am also deeply interested in psychoanalysis and have been studying at the Tavistock Clinic for some years. What I liked about his presentation was the connections made between psychoanalytic theory as I know it, and lived experience in the everyday. And this quality of it makes it much more accessible to the people I work with, an interdisciplinary team, in bereavement counselling and counselling in general practice. One particular thing came to mind, which is more by way of a question, is that I have often wondered when you wheel your baby around a supermarket, or your toddler in a pushchair, why the child lights up, in the eyes and the body, at the sight of another child, in a way that just does not happen with another adult. I have often puzzled over this. Your conception of the baby having a sense of what it is like to be itself, and also what it is like to be another person—I wondered if this sheds some light on it. Because it occurred to me that maybe it is easier to have a sense of being the other person if the other person is more like you, and perhaps this is why toddlers respond so vividly to the presence of another child.

David Tuckett

In general, I find myself in considerable agreement with what André Green has said, and his insistence on the specificity of psychoanalysis, and so on. But I thought I would content myself with picking up a few points about which I have some disquiet, arising from the response of his and others to Daniel Stern. In particular, I could not quite get André Green's point about rigour, quoting, I think, the physicist René Thom as saying that things that have been developed with rigour are not always significant, or something to that effect. Because I certainly thought that when Daniel Stern makes the point that, in his view, analysts are involved in pattern recognition, this is actually a correct point; an example has been given here with André Green's demonstration, with the discussion of the bastard from Rosine Perelberg's material, of the way in which he recognizes from a core psychoanalytic point of view certain aspects of the material. And it seems to me that part of what the discussion is about is what you feed into the core matters that you recognize, patterns that you recognize. And in this respect I think that another aspect is the distinction between hypothesis development or generation and hypothesis testing. But here I do not agree with anybody, really, because I think that some of the best work in a whole series of fields, including our own, arises from trying to think clearly about what you are looking at. I think that this is, in fact, everyday clinical work in psychoanalysis. I also think that by trying to think clearly and to do small-scale hypothesis testing, you actually develop new ideas. I have long argued (I think I wrote something twenty-one years ago) against the distinction that philosophers make—which I do not think is true of the practice of science—that is, between hypothesis testing and hypothesis generating. I think the best work involves the two being very closely linked—what I have elsewhere (Tuckett, 1994b) talked about as grounded theory!

Now in relation to this, it seems to me that one of the fundamental problems that psychoanalysis faces can be expressed in terms of Bion's idea about the overvalued idea. That is, Bion, as you will recall, describes the situation in a session where a number of things come together, click, in the analyst's mind, and something he calls the selective fact arises (Bion, 1963, p. 39; Britton & Steiner, 1994). The question then becomes: what is the difference between a selected fact and an overvalued idea which in fact is, in a sense, a delusional idea? Our discipline does have a great deal of difficulty giving up ideas, and it seems to me that proper attention to pattern recognition and to processes of hypothesis specification and testing is essential—in the session, not just in building the discipline externally—to a good-quality work that actually grows and develops and becomes more specific. Of course, the whole issue of the clinical fact is aimed at this, which I will not go into now.

One other thing I wanted to mention was the question of common sense, because, of course, my background is as a sociologist, and common sense is always something that sociologists questioned—the problem being, "common" to whom? And I think that this is one of the underlying difficulties with Daniel Stern's argument, a difficulty that has to be taken seriously. He is arguing that his work is aimed at—or, rather, that psychoanalysis ought to pay attention to—related development in so far as psychoanalytic theory and ideas coming from related developments would suggest that psychoanalysis is not obeying the laws of common sense. I think that this is a highly complicated matter, because on the one hand it must be the case that if we knowingly go against common sense in psychoanalysis, well that is one thing; but there is another more serious level of error that I think has tended to happen, where we unknowingly disagree with common sense. And at the same time we need to realize that common sense—classically and in the sociological model— has a lot to do with power and so on, and the present climate of common sense may well be profoundly anti and destructive to much of the core aspects of psychoanalysis. But I think that this comes finally to the issue of research—that it seems to me that when Irma Brenman Pick talked about research, there is some room for a form of psychoanalytic research that is more systematic than what we presently do, and more rigorous, but which is not based on, as it were, extra-psychoanalytic data.

SALLY WEINTROBE

I hope I can say what I want to say, to formulate it. I thought that I was coming to something about the tension between psychoanalytic theory, or the incompatibility between psychoanalytic theory and research, and I am finding that I do not think it is about that, certainly not what we are calling Research with a capital R in any case. But there does seem to me to be some kind of tension or some set of differences here, and I have been trying to articulate, as the time has gone on, what are they? There has been mention given to cultural differences, but I do not feel that goes far enough in explaining or articulating what these differences are; there has also been some sort of attempt to say, "well, there are not really any differences" because we can work as psychoanalysts and we can enrich our theoretical framework through all kinds of recourse to, for example, the observation of babies, which indeed is very enriching. I think my difficulty is that I am much more comfortable with André Green's viewpoint as a practising psychoanalyst, and he is really putting forward the models based on theory, and I think it is very important that it has its confines and limitations and is to do with articulating what is psychic reality. However, the tension and difference that I find is that when André Green says that psychoanalysis is not about—how did he put it?—learning to be, it makes me feel a kind of discomfort. As an analyst, I am not sure that one needs to be talking about observing infants at all to say what I am saying now, because I could just as well say what I am saying from the point of view of being an analyst with adult patients in the consulting-room. One notices all kinds of phenomena, and if one is going to say, "well, they are outside the confines of what the psychoanalytic model is", fine; but then there is a kind of tension because it is slightly limiting. Recently, at a University College Psychoanalysis Unit conference I went to, there was a very interesting moment when people were looking at the fact that something seemed to change and shift with a patient because of something that may or may not have been a technical mistake: there was a debate about this (Davies, 1999). But it seemed to be in the area of what Daniel Stern was talking about in terms of a moment when something new happens. And there are various ways in which this can happen. I saw that in Anne Alvarez' example, when she talks about a way that she helps the child to let something breathe. It is as if she sees something that is not actually articulated, and she is sensitively aware that actually it needs a space to come into being. Now, even as an analyst, it seems something slightly constricting to me, or as if it is a second-class thing: it is not really proper analysis, or it is not, if you like, a focus of legitimate enquiry. What does one do with these moments within our clinical practice? I am not talking about research or babies or anything else— I am talking about the actual consulting-room, and research in that sense. And I have not got any answers, but it seems to me that there was a danger that much as I basically agree with André Green, there could be a kind of restriction, but that there is something that Daniel Stern is referring to which I think is very important, and it is about moments of coming into being.

Elizabeth Spillius

I want to make two points—quite simple-minded ones, I think, but they have been troubling me all the way though this discussion. And one is particularly to do with Daniel Stern's formulation here, which I have also found in a book and in other papers too. I go along very nicely with the observations, and I am not for the time being bothering with the fact that I am mainly a psychoanalyst in the consulting-room, and then we get near the end of the book or near the end of the paper, and there comes a conceptualization of the observations. And I typically find the conceptualization too complex for me to understand. I would lose the link between the conceptualization and the behaviour that it is intended to clarify. Then I try again, to see if I can get my mind around it properly, and I think: will I use this in the consulting-room? Does it speak to me in that way? And generally speaking, my answer is, no, it is in a slightly different idiom, I cannot quite get it to work with the way I think analytically. And then I went back to thinking about systematic experimental infant observation, as distinct from the Tavistock Clinic psychoanalytic kind, and thought that, of necessity, it is all based on observing behaviour—behaviour of the baby, and between mother and baby usually. What does it tell us? It does not elaborate those questions—and here I very much agree with Sally Weintrobe—that I am really quite passionate to know about. I want to know crazy questions: does the baby have an unconscious? Does the baby have a recognition of me and not-me from the word go—which Klein thought, and which had always seemed obvious to me even before I read Klein—or not? And how does it develop? Is Winnicott right about the development? And similar questions. Now actually, infant observers cannot tell us this. What we really want to know, in other words, is: what goes on in the mind and the feeling part of the mind? And all they can really give is a bunch of hypotheses—it has to be, some plausible, some less plausible. But it does not tell us really, definitively, anything that we do not already know. It is very intriguing.

Then, I thought, why is it that psychoanalysts—whatever the rest of their theory is—tend to phrase it in terms of infant development? Why do they do this when they have no experience with infants except their own, and minimal bits of observation? Their experience comes from the consulting-room. Why are they so keen on such phrasing? Even Freud does this quite a bit—it is not by any means the whole of the theory, but the differentiation of an undifferentiated id, ego, and so forth. Klein does it, Anna Freud does it, Mahler does it, Winnicott does it; they do not agree with each other. But why—when all their experience really does not come from anything to do with infants, but from the consulting-room—do they phrase their theories in terms of infant development? And quite often they go from their experience in the consulting-room and extrapolate backwards, which is a considerable methodological mistake, I would think. But I am sure that it is these basic questions that we want to know about: how does the mind develop? And I am not sure that infant observation is really going to elaborate these questions about which we are so curious. It gives us new material, and it gives us some ingenious hypotheses, but it does not really address the questions that are so mysterious to us and that we so much want to know about.

JOSEPH SANDLER

I wonder, just in response to that, whether when we speak of research in infancy we are not just speaking of the observations, we are speaking of the models that are made by researchers of what goes on in the infant's mind. The question then arises of whether these have any relevance to our psychoanalytic model, and in particular to the psychoanalytic model that is implicit in our analytic work. It is not simply a question of fact that at a certain point in time the baby scratched its nose or whatever. It is not just behaviour: it is in the inferences that are drawn from it.

DANIEL STERN

Let me start with the question about common sense, because a number of things are related to this. The major part of my argument—that infancy research and observation is indirectly relevant—hangs on this business of common sense. Now, I think that there is distinction, a very important one. I do not mean what is the expectable intuition of the man on the street. I am talking about common sense from a more philosophical viewpoint, as Paul Ricoeur used when he discussed what is a hypothesis or a narrative: that is, what is known about the rest of the world and generally accepted, external to the field that you are talking about. So I am talking about what we know about the thing that is generally accepted, that is not intrinsic to psychoanalysis *per se*. That is what I mean by common sense. It is not intuition in the street. We are talking about using common sense as a point of departure with regard to what you are willing to consider and what you are less likely to consider. So I do not consider that argument really very decisive here.

This brings me to the same issue, because some, like Elizabeth Spillius, say that the infancy stuff does not tell us anything definitively, and it does not have psychoanalytic specificity. I have two things to say about that. I am not saying that the work that I do has psychoanalytic specificity. I never said that, and I am not asking for admission to the castle. What I am saying is that I am making hypotheses—and providing some data, but mostly hypotheses—and either people within the castle will find that they have some value to them, or they will not. And in that sense it has indirect relevance, because my hypotheses constitute part of the world's common sense with regard to what a baby is. I do not mean that they are good or bad—I do not know. So of course I cannot answer the question, does the baby have an unconscious? I can tell you what I would think about it, I can tell you where the possible limitations are on it, I have written very extensively on whether the baby has self–other differentiation early on on the basis of what we know—but I cannot answer it because the question that you are interested in is posed in psychoanalytic terms, with the specificity of that epistemological framework. And that is where André Green and I agree. There is no real confrontation on that point. I can give you fifty reasons why it is very unlikely that the baby will know the difference between self and other, even with great desires for fusion and whatnot, but I cannot answer that question, because it is not the kind of question that falls into the domain of my enquiry. This issue of common sense is very important here, in the terms that I am using it, otherwise there is no way that psychoanalytic discourse can have any inspiration or new ideas from any other discourse. And if it does not, then it is in trouble. It was said that some of the people here wanted to destroy psychoanalysis—I don't believe I want to destroy psychoanalysis at all. I feel that by contributing to a discourse that conceivably has indirect relevance, psychoanalysis will stay much healthier.

Let me go back to a couple of the other points, more specifically the fact that children recognize other children—I do not really have an answer for that one. It is something that has been observed so many times; even beginning at 3 months, babies seem to be recognizing other babies, as something different from anybody else, and they are very good at actually making age groupings corresponding to their own. The only possible answer that leaps to mind—I do not know whether I believe it, but at least it is plausible—is an ethnological one, similar to what Konrad Lorenz and people like that have talked about. The difference between babies' faces and adult faces is that babies' faces are constructed so that there is a human tendency to find the composition, the configuration of the face—large eyes, big forehead, small chin, small mouth, small nose, etc. and the eyes usually below the midpoint—as deaggressifying: it essentially inhibits aggression in all animal species where it has been studied, and it seems to do the same in humans. So when the baby sees another baby, there is disinhibition of any aggression and probably of fear. When a baby sees an adult face, it is in a much more problematic position, because adults in fact are dangerous to babies, and the baby should know that, the baby should be afraid, and the baby should only go towards a human face if it has those movements and configurations with which it has been slowly made familiar by virtue of exposure. In this case, it will be deaggressifized and the baby will grow comfortable, light up, and have a lot of interest. So there is a lot of sense for this position, but this is not an analytic point of view; this is what I think your average ethnologist could say about it, and I do not have any other explanation. I do not even consider that an explanation—just my associations about it.

With regard to the Esther Bick procedure, some of the time I am essentially doing an Esther Bick kind of observation, and I am very aware of myself as the observer, and frequently in a much more active way than she uses, because there the observer is much more passive. At least they do not intervene, whereas I would frequently intervene, so I was very aware of my presence and what that does to both the baby and the mother. Sometimes that is not at all the case—in fact, it is being televised and I am not even there. And I think both are valuable.

ANDRÉ GREEN

I will first reply to some of Daniel Stern's comments. About common sense: Bion wrote very interesting things about common sense, and I am afraid that they are quite different, because what Bion writes about is the community of the senses, bringing a kind of unified vision. He also talks of binocular vision. Of course, what he meant was the coexistence of consciousness and the unconscious. I am not sure that the future of psychoanalysis will rest on analysts becoming more healthy. I do not think Melanie Klein was very healthy; I do not think Bion was very healthy—he wrote about it himself, so I am not disclosing anything new. I do not think that Winnicott had ever been healthy, not to say anything of Lacan who was as mad as a hatter. But as Joseph Sandler has just said, the real issue is about infancy, not only infant observation. But I shall emphasize again, and I shall come back to Freud's words, that infancy has no privilege in Freud's work. It was one of the important parameters among others which I will not restate again, to avoid repeating what I have already said and I assume you know Freud well enough to understand that this was only one parameter. This is a very important point. How is theory formation built? Is there only one single model, or is there, to quote Daniel Stern himself quoting others, a parallel distributive processor with different axes, infancy being only of them? This is a crucial issue. It has technical implications.

I may now make some of my British friends angry. At the first Franco–British Colloquium in Brighton we heard a presentation of someone expressing great horror and saying: "I don't know what to do with this patient, because I can't make constant interpretations." The analyst was totally lost because he could not make constant interpretations, and I asked, "Why are you so troubled? Can't you wait till ____?" No—because there is such an impact here about the here-and-now technique, which is not really debated, because our conceptions of the past have to be totally changed, our conception of construction or reconstruction has to be totally reevaluated. I fully agree. But is it so certain that the here-and-now technique is the only possible way to conduct analysis? Is there not a danger of coming back to suggestion? to hypnosis? "There is just me and you in this room, and you have to listen to what I say and try to be wise. Give me exactly the answer I am waiting for." This is not a caricature; it may seem so, but when you listen to some presentations it looks very much like this.

Now to this question, to this approach, I will oppose it with a great discovery of psychoanalysis, of contemporary analysis, an epistemological one (Winnicott again)—Winnicott's discovery of the setting. This is a major, major discrepancy with the problem of infant observation or of child observation, because there is no setting. In contemporary epistemology, it is known that the way you define an object depends on the way you insulate that object—you cut it off. So the setting is really what conditions the appearance of what is an analytic object. An analytic object is not an object-relational theory. An analytic object is what takes place during the session coming from both sources, analyst and analysand. This is the potential space, which Winnicott spoke of, and which gives rise to an analytic object.

Now a word about rigour, which made David Tuckett angry. You know, there are two kinds of physicists. There are those who ask for rigour, and those who go to the extremes of rigour. If you listen to those who go to the extremes of rigour, like the Big Bang theory—I have heard a great physicist at an international meeting say, "Could it be that the world would only be an idea?" I was astonished. This is extreme rigour. And in the theories of René Thom, who created catastrophe theory—catastrophe theory having the closest links with affect—René Thom proposed two concepts: salience and pregnance. Salience is *discontinuity*. Pregnance is *diffusion*. And affect is diffusion, and it opposes the continuity and discontinuity as two forms of the mind, two forms of functioning of the mind.

Now, to end with about rigour, take again the example of Wilfred Bion. First, the middle part of his work, the grid. The grid—everything is described here (Bion, 1977). You have it all, vertical, horizontal, you can know exactly what you are, where you are at any moment. So Bion recommended the grid to be used after the session, not during it. And at a certain time, Bion said: "No grid, not any more." Why? He was Bion. He has been a prophet. He spoke of genomes before Jurassic Park. Do you realize the amount of money he could have made if he had sold the idea to Spielberg? So why? It was because Bion saw the limits of his model. And he saw that he was trying to reach something more essential, much more fundamental, and, of course, something that was responsible for all the cruelty, that savageness, the barbarity, that we all bear in ourselves.

REFERENCES

Abram, J. (Ed.) (2000). *André Green at The Squiggle Foundation.* Winnicott Studies Monograph Series. London: Karnac Books.

Ainsworth, M. D. S., Blehar, M. C., Waters, E., & Wall, S. (1978). *Patterns of Attachment: A Psychological Study of the Strange Situation.* Hillsdale, NJ: Erlbaum.

Alvarez, A. (1992). *Live Company: Psychoanalytic Psychotherapy with Autistic, Borderline, Deprived and Abused Children.* London: Routledge.

Alvarez, A., & Furgiuele, P. (1997). Speculations on components in the infant's sense of agency: the sense of abundance and the capacity to think in parentheses. In: S. Reid (Ed.), *New Developments in Infant Observation.* London: Routledge.

American Psychiatric Association (1987). *Diagnostic and Statistical Manual for Mental Disorders* (3rd edition). Washington, DC.

Atlan, H. (1994). Intentionality in Nature. *Journal for the Theory of Social Behaviour, 24* (1): 67–87.

Baldwin, J. (1895). *Mental Development in the Child and the Race.* London: Macmillan.

Beebe, B., Lachmann, F., & Jaffe, J. (1997). Mother–infant interaction structures and presymbolic self- and object-representations. *Psychoanalytic Dialogues, 7* (2): 133–182.

Bergmann, M. S. (1993). Reflections on the history of psychoanalysis. *Journal of the American Psychoanalytic Association, 41*: 929–956.

Bernfeld, S. (1925). *The Psychology of the Infant*, trans. R. Hurwitz. New York: Brentano's, 1929. London: Kegan Paul.

Bick, E. (1964). Notes on infant observation in psychoanalytic training. *International Journal of Psycho-Analysis, 45*: 558–566.

Bion, W. R. (1962). *Learning from Experience*, London: Heinemann.

Bion, W. R. (1963). *Elements of Psycho-Analysis*. London: Heinemann. [Reprinted London: Karnac Books, 1984.]

Bion, W. R. (1977). *Two Papers: The Grid and Caesura*. London: Karnac Books, 1989.

Bollas, C. (1987). *The Shadow of the Object: Psychoanalysis of the Unthought Known*. London: Free Association Books.

Borch-Jacobsen, M. (1988). *The Freudian Subject*. Stanford, CA: Stanford University Press.

Bowlby, J. (1969). *Attachment and Loss, Vol. 1: Attachment*. London: Hogarth Press & The Institute of Psycho-Analysis.

Bowlby, J. (1973). *Attachment and Loss, Vol. 2: Separation, Anxiety and Anger*. London: Hogarth Press & The Institute of Psycho-Analysis.

Bowlby, J. (1980). *Attachment and Loss, Vol. 3: Sadness and Depression*. London: Hogarth Press & The Institute of Psycho-Analysis.

Brafman, A. (1988). Infant observation. *International Review of Psycho-Analysis, 15*: 45.

Brazelton, T. B., Koslowski, B., & Main, M. (1974). The origins of reciprocity: the early mother–infant interaction. In: M. Lewis & L. A. Rosenblum (Eds.), *The Effect of the Infant on Its Caregivers*. London: Wiley Interscience.

Brenner, C. (1980). Metapsychology and psychoanalytic theory. *Psychoanalytic Quarterly, 49*: 189–215.

Britton, R., & Steiner, J. (1994). Interpretation: selected fact or overvalued idea? *International Journal of Psycho-Analysis, 75*: 1069–1078.

Bruner, J. S. (1968). *Processes of Cognitive Growth: Infancy*. Worcester, MA: Clark University Press.

Bucci, W. (1997). *Psychoanalysis and Cognitive Science: A Multiple Code Theory*. London: Guilford Press.

Bühler, C. (1928). *Kindheit und Jugend. Genese des Bewusstseins*. Leipzig: Hirzel.

Canguilhem, G. (1966). Qu'est-ce que la psychologie? In: *Les cahiers pour l'analyse, No. 1/2*. Paris: Seuil.

Chalmers, A. F. (1976). *What Is This Thing Called Science? An Assessment of the Nature and Status of Science and Its Methods: Popper, Kuhn, Lakatos, Feyerabend*. St Lucia: University of Queensland Press.

Conrad, R. (1998). Darwin's baby and baby's Darwin: mutual recognition in observational research. *Human Development, 41*: 47–64.

Cooper, A. M. (1989). Infant research and adult psychoanalysis. In: S. Dowling & A. Rothstein (Eds.), *The Significance of Infant Observational Research for Clinical Work with Children, Adolescents and Adults* (pp. 79–89). New York: International Universities Press.

Darwin, C. (1877). A biographical sketch of an infant. *Mind, 7* (July): 285.

Davies, R. (1999). Technique in the interpretation of the manifest attack on the analyst. In: R. J. Perelberg (Ed.), *Psychoanalytic Understanding of Violence and Suicide*. London: Routledge.

Donnet, J. L., & Green, A. (1973). *L'enfant de ça*. Paris: Édition de Minuit.

D'Or, J. (1988). *L'A-scientificité de la psychanalyse*. Paris: Éditions Universitaires.

Dupuy, J.-P. (1994). *Aux origines des sciences cognitives*. Paris: Éditions La Découverte.

Edelman, G. (1992). *Bright Air, Brilliant Fire: On the Matter of the Mind*. New York: Basic Books.

Edelson, M. (1977). Psychoanalysis as science. *Journal of Nervous and Mental Disorders, 165*: 1–28.

Eliot, T. S. (1943). *Four Quartets*. New York: Harcourt Brace.

Emde, R. N., & Fonagy, P. (1997). Guest Editorial. An emerging culture for psychoanalytic research? *International Journal of Psycho-Analysis, 78* (4): 643–652.

Emde, R. N., Kubicek, L., & Oppenheimer, D. (1997). Imaginative reality observed during early language development. *International Journal of Psycho-Analysis, 78*: 115–134.

Fodor, J. A. (1981). *Representations: Philosophical Essays on the Foundations of Cognitive Science*. Cambridge, MA: MIT Press.

Fodor, J. A. (1992). A theory of the child's theory of mind. *Cognition, 44*: 283–296.

Fogel, A. (1993). Two principles of communication: co-regulation and framing. In: *New Perspectives in Early Communicative Development*. London: Routledge.

Fonagy, I. (1983). *La vive voix. Essais de psycho-phonétique*. Paris: Payot.

Fonagy, P. (1982). The integration of psychoanalysis and experimental science: a review. *International Review of Psycho-Analysis, 9*: 125–145.

Fonagy, P. (1996). Discussion of Peter Wolff's paper "Infant Observation and Psychoanalysis". *Journal of the American Psychoanalytic Association, 44* (2): 404–422.

Fonagy, P. (1998). Moments of change in psychoanalytic theory: discussion of a new theory of psychic change. *Journal of Infant Mental Health, 19*: 346–393.

Fonagy, P., & Higgit, A. (1990). A developmental perspective on borderline personality disorder. *Revue Internationale de Psychopathologie, 1*: 125–160.

Fonagy, P., Steele, M., Moran, G., Steele, H., & Higgit, A. (1993). Measuring the ghost in the nursery: an empirical study of the relation between parents' mental representations of childhood experiences and their infants' security of attachment. *Journal of the American Psychoanalytic Association, 41*: 957–989.

Fonagy, P., & Tallandini-Shallice, M. (1993). Problems of psychoanalytic research in practice. *Bulletin of The Anna Freud Centre, 16* (Part 1): 5–22.

Freud, S. (1905c). Jokes and their relation to the unconscious. *S.E., 8*.

Freud, S. (1905d). *Three Essays on the Theory of Sexuality. S.E., 7*.

Freud, S. (1909d). Notes upon a case of obsessional neurosis. *S.E., 10*.

Freud, S. (1909b). Analysis of a phobia in a five-year-old boy. *S.E., 10*.

Freud, S. (1915e). The unconscious. *S.E., 14*.

Freud, S. (1918b [1914]). From the history of an infantile neurosis. *S.E., 17*.

Freud, S. (1919e). A child is being beaten. *S.E., 10*.

Freud, S. (1920g). *Beyond the Pleasure Principle. S.E., 17*.

Freud, S. (1923d). *The Ego and the Id. S.E., 19*.

Freud, S. (1925f). Preface to Aichhorn's *Wayward Youth. S.E., 19*.

Freud, S. (1926d [1925]). *Inhibitions, Symptoms and Anxiety. S.E., 20*.

Freud, S. (1926e). *The Question of Lay Analysis. S.E., 20*.

Freud, S. (1926f [1925]). Psycho-analysis. *S.E., 20*.

Freud, S. (1933a). *New Introductory Lectures on Psycho-Analysis. S.E., 22.*

Freud, S. (1950 [1895]). A project for a scientific psychology. *S.E., 1.*

Gabbard, G. (1995). The emerging common ground. *International Journal of Psycho-Analysis, 76*: 475–486.

Gay, P. (1988). *Freud: A Life for Our Time.* London: J. M. Dent.

Godelier, M. (1958). *Rationalite et irrationalite en economie.* Paris: Librairie Francois Maspero.

Green, A. (1962). L'Inconscient freudian et la psychanalyse francaise contemporaine. *Les Temps Modernes,* 195: 365–370.

Green, A. (1973). *Le discours vivant. La conception psychanalytique de l'affect.* Paris: Presses Universitaires de France.

Green, A. (1979). L'enfant modèle. *Nouvelle Revue de Psychanalyse, 19*: 27–47.

Green, A. (1983). *Narcissisme de vie, Narcissisme de mort.* Paris: Les Editions de Minuit.

Green, A. (1986a). The dead mother. In: *On Private Madness* (pp. 86–135). London: Hogarth Press & The Institute of Psycho-Analysis.

Green, A. (1986b). *On Private Madness.* London: Hogarth Press & The Institute of Psycho-Analysis. [Reprinted London: Karnac Books, 1997.]

Green, A. (1986c). Psychoanalysis and ordinary modes of thought. In: *On Private Madness.* London: Hogarth Press & The Institute of Psycho-Analysis. [Reprinted London: Karnac Books, 1997.]

Green, A. (1991). *Méconnaissance de l'inconscient et la science,* edited by R. Dorey. Paris: Éditions Dounod.

Green, A. (1992). A propos de l'observation des bébés. *Journal de la Psychanalyse de l'Enfant, 12*: 133–153.

Green, A. (1993a). Discussion of the inner experience of the analyst. *International Journal of Psycho-Analysis, 74* (6): 1131–1136.

Green, A. (1993b). *Le travail du negatif.* Paris: Les Editions de Minuit.

Green, A. (1995). *La causalité psychique.* Paris: Odile Jacob.

Green, A. (1999a). *The Fabric of Affect in the Psychoanalytic Discourse.* London: Routledge.

Green, A. (1999b). *The Work of the Negative.* London & New York: Free Association Books.

Gunderson, J. G. (1984). *Borderline Personality Disorder.* Washington, DC: American Psychoanalytic Association.

Heimann, P. (1944). Discussion held on the 16th February 1944 on

P. Heimann and S. Isaacs "On Regression". In: P. King & R. Steiner (Eds.), *The Freud–Klein Controversies, 1941–45* (pp. 730–751). London: Routledge & The Institute of Psycho-Analysis, 1992.

Hobson, P. (1992). "Responses to Professor Daniel Stern's paper 'Phantasy from a Developmental Perspective'." Unpublished paper.

Hobson, P. (1993). *Autism and the Development of Mind*. London: Erlbaum.

Hug-Hellmuth, H. von. (1913). *A Study of the Mental Life of the Child*, trans. J. Putnam & M. Stevens. Washington, DC: Nervous & Mental Disease Company, 1919.

Hurry, A. (Ed.) (1998). *Psychoanalysis and Developmental Therapy*. London: Karnac Books.

Husserl, E. (1964). *The Phenomenology of Internal Time–Consciousness*, edited by M. Heidegger. Bloomington, IN: Indiana University Press.

Isaacs, S. (1943). The nature and the function of phantasy. In: P. King & R. Steiner (Eds.), *The Freud–Klein Controversies, 1941–45* (pp. 264–321). London: Routledge & The Institute of Psycho-Analysis, 1992.

Jakobson, R. (1990). *On Language*, edited by L. R. Waugh & M. Monville-Burston. Cambidge, MA: Harvard University Press.

Jones, E. (1957). *Sigmund Freud: Life and Work, Vol. 2*. London: Hogarth Press.

Joseph, B. (1985). Transference: the total situation. *International Journal of Psycho-Analysis, 66*: 447–454.

Kernberg, O. (1985). Neurosis, psychosis and the borderline states. In: H. I. Kaplan & B. J. Saddock (Eds.), *Comprehensive Textbook of Psychiatry* (pp. 621–630). Baltimore, MD: Williams & Wilkins.

King, P., & Steiner, R. (Eds.) (1992). *The Freud–Klein Controversies, 1941–45*. London: Routledge & The Institute of Psycho-Analysis.

Klein, M. (1944). The emotional life and ego development of the infant with special reference to the depressive position. In: P. King & R. Steiner, *The Freud–Klein Controversies, 1941–45* (pp. 752–797). London: Routledge & The Institute of Psycho-Analysis, 1992.

Kohon, G. (1999). *The Dead Mother. The Work of André Green*. London: Routledge.

Kris, E. (1956). The recovery of childhood memories in psycho-analysis. *Psychoanalytic Study of the Child, 11*: 54–88.

Lacan, J. (1977). The mirror stage as formative of the function of the I.

In: *Ecrits: A Selection*, trans. A. Sheridan. London: Tavistock Publications.

Laplanche, J. (1997). The theory of seduction and the problem of the other. *International Journal of Psycho-Analysis, 78*: 653–666.

Laplanche, J., & Pontalis, J.-B. (1973). *The Language of Psychoanalysis*. London: Hogarth Press and The Institute of Psychoanalysis. [Reprinted London: Karnac Books, 1988.]

Lazar, R., Ropke, C., & Ermann, G. (1998). Learning to be: on the observation of a premature baby. *Infant Observation: The International Journal of Infant Observation and Its Applications, 2* (1): 21–39.

Lévi-Strauss, C. (1971). *L'Homme nu*. Paris: Plon.

Macey, D. (1988). *Lacan in Context*. London: Verso.

Mahler, M., Pine, F., & Bergman, A. (1975). *The Psychological Birth of the Human Infant*. New York: Basic Books. [Reprinted London: Karnac Books, 1991.]

Main, M., Kaplan, N., & Cassidy, J. (1985). Security in infancy, childhood and adulthood: a move to the level of representation. In: I. Bretherton & E. Waters (Eds.), *Growing Points of Attachment Theory and Research*. Monographs of the Society for Research in Child Development (pp. 66–104), Serial no. 209, 50 (1–2). Chicago, IL: University of Chicago Press.

Middlemore, M. (1942). *The Nursing Couple*. London: Hamish Hamilton.

Miller, L., Rustin, M., Rustin, M., & Shuttleworth, J. (1989). *Closely Observed Infants*. London: Duckworth.

Morin, E. (1991). *La Méthode, 4: Les idées, leur habitat, leur vie, leurs moeurs, leur organisation*. Paris: Éditions Seuil.

Murray, L., & Cooper, P. J. (1997). The role of infant and maternal factors in postpartum depression: mother–infant outcomes and infant outcome. In: L. Murray & P. J. Cooper (Eds.), *Postpartum Depression and Child Development*. New York: Guilford Press.

Olds, D., & Cooper, A. M. (1997). Guest Editorial. Dialogue with other sciences: opportunities for mutual gain. *International Journal of Psycho-Analysis, 78*: 219–226.

Perelberg, R. J. (1999a). *Psychoanalytic Understanding of Violence and Suicide*. New Library of Psychoanalysis, No. 33. London: Routledge.

Perelberg, R. J. (1999b). The interplay between identifications and identity in the analysis of a violent young man. *International Journal of Psycho-Analysis, 80* (1): 31–45.

Peterfreund, E. (1978). Some critical comments on psychoanalytic conceptualizations of infancy. *International Journal of Psycho-Analysis, 59*: 427–441.

Popper, K. (1959). *The Logic of Scientific Discovery*. London: Routledge, 1992.

Preyer, W. (1882). *The Mind of the Child, Vols. I and II*. New York/ London: Appleton and Company.

Reid, S. (Ed.) (1997). *Developments in Infant Observations*. London: Routledge.

Ricoeur, P. (1970). *Freud and Philosophy: An Essay in Interpretation*. New Haven, CT: Yale University Press.

Ricoeur, P. (1977). The question of proof in Freud's psychoanalytic writings. *Journal of the American Psychoanalytic Association, 25*: 835–871.

Rilke, R. M. (1958). *The Notebooks of Malte Laurids Brigge*. New York: Capricorn Books.

Robinson, P. (1993). *Freud and His Critics*. Berkeley, CA: University of California Press.

Rosenfeld, H. (1987). *Impasse and Interpretation. New Library of Psycho-Analysis*. London: Routledge.

Roudinesco, E. (1993). *Jacques Lacan. Esquisse d'une vie, historie d'un système de pensée*. Paris: Fayard.

Rustin, M. (1989). Observing infants: reflections on methods. In: L. Miller, M. Rustin, M. Rustin, & J. Shuttleworth, *Closely Observed Infants*. London: Duckworth.

Rustin, M. (1997). What do we see in the nursery? Infant observation as "laboratory work". *Infant Observation: The International Journal of Infant Observation and Its Applications 1* (1): 93–110.

Sandler, J. (1976a). Dreams, unconscious phantasy and identity of perception. *International Review of Psycho-Analysis, 3*: 33–42.

Sandler, J. (1976b). Countertransference and role-responsiveness. *International Review of Psycho-Analysis, 3*: 43–47.

Sandler, J. (1983). Reflections on some relations between psychoanalytic concepts and psychoanalytic practice. *International Journal of Psycho-Analysis, 64*: 35–45.

Sandler, J. (1998). A generative grammar of phantasy. Some thoughts on H. Segal's paper "Phantasy and Reality". *British Psychoanalytical Society Bulletin, 35* (6, 1999): 23.

Sandler, J., Holder, A., Dare, C., & Dreher, A. U. (1997). *Freud's Models of the Mind: An Introduction*. London: Karnac Books; Madison, CT: International Universities Press.

Sandler, J., & Sandler, A.-M. (1983). The "second censorship", the "three-box model" and some technical implications. *International Journal of Psycho-Analysis, 64*: 413–425.

Sandler, J., & Sandler, A.-M. (1984). The past unconscious and the present unconscious and the interpretation of the transference. *Psychoanalytic Enquirer, 4*: 367.

Sandler, J., & Sandler, A.-M. (1987). The past unconscious, the present unconscious and the vicissitudes of guilt. *International Journal of Psycho-Analysis, 68*: 337.

Sandler, J., & Sandler, A.-M. (1994). The past unconscious, the present unconscious and interpretation of the transference. *Psychoanalytic Study of the Child, 49*: 278–292.

Schore, A. N. (1997). Early organization of the nonlinear right brain and development of a predisposition to psychiatric disorders. *Development and Psychopathology, 9* (4): 595–631.

Segal, H. (1957). Notes on symbol formation. *International Journal of Psycho-Analysis, 38*: 391–397.

Segal, H. (1978). On symbolism. *International Journal of Psycho-Analysis, 59*: 315–319.

Segal, H. (1999). Unpublished paper given at the Joseph Sandler Memorial Meeting organized by the Research Committee of the Insitute of Psycho-Analysis, University College, London (May).

Spence, D. P. (1982). Narrative truth and theoretical truth. *Psychoanalytic Quarterly, 51*: 43–69.

Steiner, R. (1984). Review of "Psychoanalysis in France" edited by S. Lebovici & D. Widlocher. *International Journal of Psycho-Analysis, 65:* 232.

Steiner, R. (1987). Review of André Green's "Narcissisme de vie, Narcissisme de mort". *International Journal of Psycho-Analysis, 88*: 133.

Steiner, R. (1995). Hermeneutics or Hermes-mess? *International Journal of Psycho-Analysis, 76* (Part 3): 435–445.

Steiner, R. (1998). Unpublished paper given at J. Sandler's invitation at the launching of J. & A.-M. Sandler's book, *Internal Objects Revisited*, The Anna Freud Centre (July).

Steiner, R. (in press). *The Importance of the Cultural Extra-Analytical Background of the Freud–Klein Controversial Discussions (1941–45).* London: Karnac Books.

Stern, D. (1977). Missteps in the dance. In: *The First Relationship: Infant and Mother*. Cambridge, MA: Harvard University Press.

Stern, D. (1985). *The Interpersonal World of the Infant*. New York: Basic Books. [Reprinted London: Karnac Books, 1998.]

Stern, D. (1992a). "The Pre-Narrative Envelope: An Alternative View of Unconscious Phantasy in Infancy." Paper presented at symposium in memory of George Moran, London.

Stern, D. (1992b). Considerations of unconscious phantasy from a developmental perspective. *British Psychoanalytical Society Bulletin*.

Stern, D. (1994). One way to build a clinically relevant baby. *Infant Mental Health Journal, 15*: 9–25.

Stern, D. (1995a). Ce que comprend le bébé. In: O. Bourguignon & M. Bydlowsky (Eds.), *La recherche clinique en biologie*. Paris: Presses Universitaires de France.

Stern, D. (1995b). *The Motherhood Constellation*. New York: Basic Books. [Reprinted London: Karnac Books, 1998.]

Sullivan, H. S. (1953). *The Interpersonal Theory of Psychiatry*. New York: Norton.

Symington, J. (1997). The little obsessional alchemist. *Journal of Child Psychotherapy, 23* (2): 265–278.

Thom, R. (1968). La science malgré tout. *Encyclopedie Universale, 17*: 5–10.

Trevarthen, C. (1977). Descriptive analyses of infant communicative behaviour. In: H. R. Shaffer (Ed.), *Studies in Mother–Infant Interaction*. London: Academic Press.

Trevarthen, C. (1987). Sharing makes sense: intersubjectivity and the making of an infant's meaning. In: R. Steele & T. Threadgold (Eds.), *Language Topics: Essays in Honour of Michael Halliday*. Philadelphia, PA: John Benjamins.

Trevarthen, C., & Hubley, P. (1978). Secondary intersubjectivity: confidence, confiding and acts of meaning in the first year. In: A. Lock (Ed.), *Action, Gesture and Symbol: The Emergence of Language*. London: Academic Press.

Tronick, E. Z., & Cohn, J. F. (1989). Infant–mother face-to-face interaction: age and gender differences in coordination and the occurrence of miscoordination. *Child Development, 60*: 85–92.

Tuckett, D. (1994a). The conceptualization and communication of clinical facts in psychoanalysis. *International Journal of Psycho-Analysis, 75*: 865–870.

Tuckett, D. (1994b). Developing a grounded hypothesis to understand a clinical process: the role of conceptualisation in validation. *International Journal of Psycho-Analysis, 75*: 1159–1180.

Tustin, F. (1981). *Autistic States in Children*. London: Routledge & Kegan Paul.

Tustin, F. (1988). Psychotherapy with children who cannot play. *International Journal of Psycho-Analysis, 15*: 93–106.

Varela, F. J. (1984). Introduction. In: H. Von Foerster, *Observing Systems*. Seaside, CA: Intersystems Publications.

Vaughan, S., & Roose, S. P. (1995). The analytic process: clinical and research definitions. *International Journal of Psycho-Analysis, 76* (2): 343–356.

Vidal, J.-M. (1993). Discontinuities psychiques entres animaux et humains: eclairage sur la "monade autistique" [Psychic discrepancies between animals and humans: illumination of the "autistic monad"]. *Psychiatrie de l'enfant, 36* (1): 67–87.

Von Foerster, H. (1984). *Observing Systems* (2nd edition). Seaside, CA: Intersystems Publications.

Wallerstein, R. S. (1986). *Forty-two Lives in Treatment: A Study of Psychoanalysis and Psychotherapy*. New York: Guilford Press.

Wallerstein, R. S. (1988). One psychoanalysis or many. *International Journal of Psycho-Analysis, 69* (1): 1.

Wallerstein, R. S., & Sampson, H. (1971). Issues in research in the psychoanalytic process. *International Journal of Psycho-Analysis, 52*: 11–50.

Wallon, H. (1949). *Origines du charactère chez l'enfant: les préludes du sentiment de la personnalité*. Paris: Presses Universitaires de France.

Widlöcher, D. (1994). A case is not a fact. *International Journal of Psycho-Analysis, 75* (1): 233–244.

Winnicott, D. W. (1949). Hate in the countertransference. *International Journal of Psycho-Analysis, 30*: 69–74. Also in: *Collected Papers: Through Paediatrics to Psycho-Analysis*. London: Tavistock, 1958.

[Reprinted as *Through Paediatrics to Psycho-Analysis*. London: Hogarth Press & The Institute of Psycho-Analysis, 1975; reprinted London: Karnac Books, 1990.]

Winnicott, D. W. (1953). Transitional objects and transitional phenomena. In: *Collected Papers: Through Paediatrics to Psycho-Analysis*. London: Tavistock, 1958. [Reprinted as *Through Paediatrics to Psycho-Analysis*. London: Hogarth Press & The Institute of Psycho-Analysis, 1975; reprinted London: Karnac Books, 1990.]

Winnicott, D. W. (1956). Primary maternal preoccupation. In: *Collected Papers: Through Paediatrics to Psycho-Analysis*. London: Tavistock, 1958. [Reprinted as *Through Paediatrics to Psycho-Analysis*. London: Hogarth Press & The Institute of Psycho-Analysis, 1975; reprinted London: Karnac Books, 1990.]

Winnicott, D. W. (1957). On the contribution of direct child observation to psycho-analysis. In: *The Maturational Processes and the Facilitating Environment*. London: Hogarth Press & The Institute of Psycho-Analysis, 1965. [Reprinted London: Karnac Books, 1990.]

Winnicott, D. W. (1960). Ego distortion in terms of true and false self. In: *The Maturational Processes and the Facilitating Environment*. London: Hogarth Press & The Institute of Psycho-Analysis, 1965. [Reprinted London: Karnac Books, 1990.]

Winnicott, D. W. (1971). *Therapeutic Consultations in Child Psychiatry*. London: Hogarth Press & The Institute of Psycho-Analysis.

Wolff, P. H. (1996). The irrelevance of infant observation for psychoanalysis. *Journal of the American Psychoanalytic Association*, 44: 369–473.

INDEX

Abraham, K., 24
Abram, J., 3
absence, 35, 66, 82, 86–90
  of negation, 95
actualization, 109
affect(s), 4, 34, 86, 126, 131, 141
aggression, 64, 125, 139
Aichhorn, A., 63
Ainsworth, M. D. S., 87
alpha function, 65, 104
Alvarez, A., xiii, 1, 2, 100–107, 119, 120, 122, 135
American Psychiatric Association, DSM-III-R, 99
analogy, 59, 61, 67, 93
  and metaphor, 57
analytic eye, 15
analytic object, 141
analytic setting, 4, 33, 46, 51, 52, 55, 66, 71, 99, 141
  language of, 61
analytic situation, 68, 92
  and analytic setting, 24
  and empirical science, 27, 63–64
Anlehnung, 64
Anna Freud Centre, xv, 8
  Young Adults Research Scheme, 98
après coup [Nachträglichkeit, deferred action], 4, 5, 13, 14, 48, 63, 81–85, 93, 97, 99, 124, 127, 128, 130
  see also: coup
Aristotle, 65
Atlan, H., 23, 55
attachment:
  theory, 69, 116, 129
  transgenerational patterns of, 97
autistic children, 67, 101, 105
avant coup, 84
  see also: après coup; coup

Baldwin, J., 11, 12
Barkay, P., xvii
Barratt, B. B., 42
basic assumption, 45, 125
Beebe, B., 103
behaviour, 126
  model of, 50

behaviourism, 6, 8, 47, 54, 76, 98, 114, 124
Bergman, A., 24, 35, 59
Bergmann, M. S., 49
Bernfeld, S., 11, 13
Bick, E., 6, 8, 12, 108, 109, 131, 139
binocular vision, 140
biology, 14, 29, 44
Bion, W. R., 5, 24, 58, 69, 71, 103
  on alpha function, 104
  on binocular vision, 95, 140
  on common sense, 115, 140
  container/contained model of, 34, 108
  on dream as paradigm, 63
  grid of, 65, 141–142
  on Keats's negative capability, 55
  on maternal reverie, 55
  on overvalued idea, 133
  on preconception, 104
  on reality, handling of, 52
  on selective fact, 133
  theory of mind of, 49
  on thinking, 120
  on unthinkable thoughts, 104
Blehar, M. C., 87
Bollas, C., 89, 104
Bonaparte, M., 16
Borch-Jacobsen, M., 61
borderline children, 101, 104
Boston Psychoanalytic Institute, 42
Bowlby, J., 35, 69, 116, 128, 129
Braten, S., 8
Brazelton, T. B., 96, 97
breast:
  intrusive, 112
  suffocating, 114–115
Brenman Pick, I., xiv, 1–3, 8, 108–118, 120, 123, 125, 134
Brenner, C., 55
Brentano, F., 7
Brierley, M., 14
British Psycho-Analytical Society, 95, 98, 131
British school of object relations, 6
Britton, R., xvii, 133
Bruner, J. S., 102, 104, 105, 106
Bucci, W., 101
Bühler, C., 12

Canguilhem, G., 98
case studies, 94–97, 116–118
Cassidy, J., 97
catastrophe theory, 141
censorship, 95
Chalmers, A. F., 23
child, as paradigm for psychoanalysis, 63–64
chronic traumatic stress disorder, 101
chronos, 83
  see also: temporality; time
Churchland, P. M., 55
clinical facts, 25, 29
clinical setting, 4, 24, 33, 46, 51, 52, 55, 63, 66, 71, 92, 99, 141
  language of, 61
cognitivism, 9, 24, 47
Cohn, J. F., 87
common sense, 92, 115, 134, 137, 138, 140
  see also: plausibility
concept, 57
Conrad, R., 11
construction, 141
container/contained, 34, 108
Cooper, A. M., 15, 43
Cooper, P. J., 113
core self, 10
cotton reel (*fort–da*) game, 62, 64–66
countertransference, 34, 104, 108, 112
  hate in, 108
coup, 6, 82, 87
Crick, F., 55
cultural differences, 3, 5, 10, 55, 120, 128, 135

Dare, C., 48
Darwin, C., 11, 12, 47
Davidson, A., 55
Davies, R., xiv, xvii–xviii, 2, 135
decentration, 88
deferred action, *see: après coup*
  see also: avant coup; coup
Dennett, D. C., 55
depressive position, 12
desire, 28, 29, 51, 86

Freudian–Lacanian concept of, 55
vs. motivation, 25, 30
development, as paradigm for psychoanalysis, 101
developmental stages, 112
Diamond, N., 127, 132
Donnet, J.-L., 44
D'Or, J., 98
drama, 57
dream:
as paradigm for psychoanalysis, 63–64, 100, 119
work, 33, 63
Dreher, A. U., 48
drive [*Trieb, pulsion*]:
vs. instinct, 5
vs. motivation, 55
nature of, 87
and phonation, 62
and representation, 34, 129
role of, 8, 51
self-preservative, 64
sexual, 64
theory, 4, 8, 25, 36, 49, 126, 129
DSM-III-R (American Psychiatric Association), 99
Dupuy, J.-P., 23
dynamic point of view, 51, 126
dynamic template, 98
dynamic unconscious, 121, 122

early infantile phantasies, 121
early object relationship, 6, 11, 115
Eccles, J., 55
Eckstein, F., 12
economic point of view, 51
Edelman, G., 47, 55
Edelson, M., 61, 98
ego, 8, 24, 121, 122, 126
Freudian concepts of, 25
origin of, 60
psychology, 6, 24, 43, 64
structure of, and id, 49
undifferentiated, 137
Eliot, T. S., 53
Emde, R. N., 5, 43–45, 52, 54, 59, 64–67, 109
emergent self, 10
empathy, 56
empirical scientific method, 77
enactment, 43
enumerative induction, 57
epistemology, 23, 44, 53, 55, 69, 71, 141
Ermann, G., 103, 104
evenly suspended attention, 66, 67, 78, 102

false self, 129
femininity, three generations of, 69–72
Ferenczi, S., 24, 110
Fields Medal, 47
Flechsig, P. E., 11
Fodor, J. A., 47
Fogel, A., 103
Fonagy, I., 61, 62
Fonagy, P., xvii–xviii, 2, 5, 24, 42–44, 54, 59, 61, 62, 64, 66, 97–99, 109
fort–da (cotton-reel) game, 62, 64–65, 66
fragmentation, 103
Frankl, G., 12
free association, 4, 33, 66, 67, 68
free-floating attention, 66, 67, 78, 102
Freud, A., 12–14, 51, 58, 129, 137
Anna Freud Centre, xv, 8
Freud–Klein Controversial Discussions, 13, 14
Freud, S.:
clinical views of, 4
"cooperation of the two methods", 1
Little Hans, 50
metapsychology of, 4
Nachträglichkeit ["deferred action", *"après coup"*], 4, 5, 13, 14, 63, 81
phylogenetic traces, 22
primary narcissism, 4
psychoanalysis as science, 22
Rat Man, 50
temporality, 4, 7
theory of drives of, 4
"unconscious", 4

Freudian concepts of the ego, 25
Freudian–Lacanian concept of desire, 55
Friedlander, K., 14
Furgiuele, P., 106

Gabbard, G., 43
Gay, P., 16
Geissmann, P., 3
genetic continuity, 14, 15, 65
genetic pre-structure, 57
Godelier, M., 98
Green, A., *passim*
grid [Bion], 65, 141–142
Gunderson, J. G., 99
Gunther, M., 114, 115

hallucinatory wish-fulfilment, 60
Hartmann, H., 12, 24, 49, 58, 64
Heimann, P., 14, 15
Hellmann, I., 12
here-and-now technique, 141
Higgit, A., 97
historical truth, 129
Hobson, P., 95, 97
Holder, A., 48
Hubley, P., 87, 102
Hug-Hellmuth, H. von, 11
Hurry, A., 8
Husserl, E., 7, 83, 85
hypercomplexity, 23, 29, 34, 69, 103
hypothesis:
  generation, 8, 76, 78–80, 102, 133
  testing, 8, 74, 76, 79, 80, 102, 133, 134

id, 25, 48, 49, 51, 83, 121, 126
  vs. unconscious, 120
  undifferentiated, 137
imaginative reality, 52, 55
indeterminacy, 23, 29
infancy, vs. infant observation, 140
infantile, 7, 11
  vs. infant, 4, 50–54, 92, 93
  unconscious as, 51, 93
infantile amnesia, 121
infantile narcissism, 60
inference:
  clinical, 11
  hypothetical, 13
  scientific, 29
insight, 101
instinct, 49, 55
instinctual impulse, representation, 126
intentionality, 7, 25
  vs. desire, 30
  longitudinal, 85
interactive view, 49
internal object, 95, 98
International Psychoanalytical Association (IPA), 6, 26, 44, 48, 54, 64, 109
interpersonal, the, concept of, 49
interpersonal relationship, 24, 25, 118
  infant–mother, 4
interpersonal subjective experience, 52
interpersonal view, 49
interpersonal world, 24, 25
  of infant, 4, 86, 92, 114, 118
interpretation, 89
intersubjective:
  concept of, 25, 43, 49, 64, 88–89, 103
  experience, 69
    infant's, 88
    patient–analyst, 89
intrapsychic:
  concept of, 4, 24, 25, 35, 50, 92
  life, 4, 14, 15, 24, 114, 118
  processes, 60, 86, 92
  structures, 69
  work, 69
IPA, *see:* International Psychoanalytical Association
Isaacs, S., 12, 14, 64

Jaffe, J., 103
Jakobson, R., 59, 62
Jones, E., 16
Joseph, B., 108

Kaplan, N., 97
Keats, J., 55

Kernberg, O., 99
King, P., 12, 14
Klein, M., 5, 8, 15, 24, 58, 59, 63, 69, 71, 113–115, 136, 137, 140
  Controversial Discussions, 13, 14
  early object relationships, 6, 11–12, 115
knowledge, 127, 128
  explicit, 89
  implicit, 88, 89, 104, 122
Kohon, G., 3, 148
Kohut, H., 64
Koslowski, B., 96
Kris, E., 53
Kubicek, L., 45

Lacan, J., 5, 6, 12, 24, 64, 65, 128, 140
Lachmann, F., 103
language, 53, 126, 127, 130
  development, 96
    and metaphor, 61
    phases of, 14
    phonemes in, 62
  music as, 7, 93
  role of in psychoanalysis, 4, 7, 61
Laplanche, J., 47, 98
lava-flow metaphor, 128
Lazar, R., 103, 104
Leach, K., xviii
leaning (*Anlehnung*), 64
Lebovici, S., 58, 66
Lévi-Strauss, C., 93, 124
Little Hans, 50
Lorenz, K., 139

Macey, D., 12
Mahler, M., 24, 35, 59, 66, 79, 137
Main, M., 96, 97
meaning:
  reversal of, 33
  unconscious, 129
mechanisms of defence, 33
memory, 68, 71, 82, 84, 87, 89, 98, 114
  amnesic, 129
  primary, 83
metaphor, 59–62, 65, 95, 106, 120, 128
  and analogy, 57
  living, 56
  polysemic, 71
metapsychology:
  Freudian, 49, 57, 74
    and empirical research, 59–62
    systematic demolition of, 60
    as witch, 57
  metaphors in, 62
  psychoanalytic, 25, 30
    developmental, 88, 90
Middlemore, M., 12
Miller, A., xiv
Miller, L., 8, 102
mirror stage, 12
mnemic reverberations, 71
model of mind:
  structural, 49, 104, 121–122, 126
  topographical, 24, 51, 104, 121, 122, 125
moment, 127
Morin, E., 23
Morra, M., 131–132
mother:
  –infant interaction, 76, 77, 93, 96, 125
  internal, 112
motivation, 56, 85
  Anglo-Saxon psychological concept of, 55
  vs. desire, 25, 30, 55
  vs. drive, 55
motives, hidden, concept of, 48
movement, 77, 78, 96, 101, 120, 124–126, 139
Murray, L., 113
music, 6, 7, 57, 84–86, 91–93, 124, 126

Nachträglichkeit, see: après coup
  see also: avant coup; coup
narcissism:
  destructive, 108
  primary, 4, 11, 82, 88
narrative, 56, 68, 71, 74, 75, 138
narrative envelope, 56, 57
  pre-, 54
  proto-, 54, 57
narrative truth, 68

natural science, 7, 8, 29
psychology as, 36
negative capability [Keats], 55
neurobiology, 56
neuroscience, 9, 47
neurotic defence, 112
"now", issue of, 82–90, 120, 124, 129, 130
nursing couple, 12

objectivism, 33, 44, 50, 60
anti-, 3
object relations, 69
British school of, 6
of infants, 11, 80, 115
inner subjective world of, 123
primitive, 97
theory, 25, 64, 103
observable interaction, 4
Oedipus, 7
complex, 4, 111
Olds, D., 43
omnipotence, 60
omnipotent phantasies, 96
Oppenheimer, D., 45
orality, 24
oral phase, 64
overvalued idea, 133–134

parallel distributed processing, 56
paranoid–schizoid position, 115
Paris Psycho-Analytical Society, 91
past horizon, 83, 84
Pasteur, L., 104
past unconscious, 15, 69, 89
pattern recognition, 78, 133
Paulhan, J., 41
perception, 14, 57, 86
and action, duality of, 50
infant's, 114, 115, 118
theory of, 58
Perelberg, R. J., xiv, 1, 3, 91–99, 120, 124, 133
personality, theory of, 24
Peterfreund, E., 59, 60, 61
phantasy(ies), 87, 98
life of child, 13
philosophy:
of mind, 69
of science, 47
phonation, 62
phonology, 61
phylogenetic traces, 22
physiology, 46
Piaget, J., xiv, 8, 12, 56, 88
Pierce, C. S., 126
Pine, F., 24, 35, 59
place-holding, 105
plausibility, 75, 77, 78, 90
see also: common sense
play, 53, 101, 120
pleasure–unpleasure principle, 51
poetry, 57
Pontalis, J.-B., 98
Popper, K., 46
post-traumatic stress disorder, 101
potential space, 141
preconception, 104
preconscious, 25, 30, 36, 65, 104, 121, 122
predetermined epigenesis, 57
pregnance [Thom], 141
pre-narrative envelope, 54
pre-object, 57
pre-psychoanalytic psychology, 25
presence, 35, 82, 86–90, 95, 132, 140
presentation:
thing, 34, 56, 57, 95
word, 56, 57
present unconscious, 15, 63, 68
pretence, 65
pre-thinking, 57
Preyer, W., 11, 12
primal fantasies, 121, 129
primary memory, 83
primary narcissism, 4, 11, 82, 88
primary process, 68
primary unconscious phantasy(ies), 14
primordial impression, 83
projection, 4, 10, 56, 78, 103, 118
projective identification, 43, 56, 65, 95, 108
protention, 83, 85

proto-narrative, 57, 104
envelopes, 54
psychiatry, 46
psychic apparatus, concepts of, 34, 36, 49
psychic organization and separation anxiety, 35
psychic process, 34, 82
psychic reality, 4, 30, 52, 54, 64, 66, 67, 135
psychic work, 33, 81, 87
psychoanalysis:
attacks on, 45
empirical basis of, 62
vs. psychology, 24, 30, 36, 49, 55
scientificity of, 22
spirit of, 26–28, 32, 76, 80, 102
psychoanalytic identity, 32, 36
psychoanalytic state of mind, 4, 45, 63
psychology, 46
cognitive, 47
depth, 30, 49
general, psychoanalytic theory as, 49
pre-psychoanalytic, 25
and psychic activity, 48–72
and psychoanalysis, 24, 30, 36, 49, 55
psychoanalytic, 24, 31, 42
scientific, 59
two-body, 49
Psychotherapy Research Project of the Menninger Foundation, 29
psychotic children, 34, 104, 105
psychotic defence, 112
psychotic patients, 52
pulsion, see: drive

Rank, O., 24
Raphael-Leff, J., xiv, 2
Rat Man, 50
reality:
principle, 29, 51
testing, 114
reconstruction, 141
reflective function, 97
regression, 14, 71, 129
Reid, S., xiii, 97
reparation, 65
repetition compulsion, 129
representation, 28, 33, 34, 54, 58, 66, 80, 129, 131
affect, 56
of being-with object, 88
building of, 56
channels of, 51
as form, 126
infant's, 87, 89
instinctual impulse, 126
and intersubjectivity, 88–89
model of, vs. model of behaviour, 50
symbolic, 97
repression, 33, 34, 63, 89, 95, 121
concept of, 48
resistance, 33
retention, 83, 85
reverie, maternal, 55, 65
reversal of meaning, 33
Ricoeur, P., 47, 56, 75, 138
rigour, 5, 47, 133, 141
Rilke, R. M., 101, 102
Robinson, P., 98
Roose, S. P., 23
Ropke, C., 103, 104
Rosenfeld, H., 5, 52, 108
Rosenzweig, S., 16
Roudinesco, E., 12
Rustin, M., 8, 100, 102, 104

Sacerdoti, C., xvii, 2
salience [Thom], 141
Sandler, A.-M., xiv, xvii–xviii, 2, 15, 58, 63, 68, 89, 97, 98
Sandler, J., xv, xvii, xviii
and actualization, 109
and concept of infancy, 58
and past and present unconscious, 15, 63, 68–69, 89, 97, 98
and research in infancy, 15, 137
and use of term "unconscious", 121–122, 126
Schore, A. N., 103

scientific inference, 29
scientific method, role of in psychoanalysis, 47
screen:
memories, 26
training, 26, 48
scripts, 57
Searles, H., 5, 52
secondary process, 68
Segal, H., 15, 52, 108
selective fact, 133–134
self:
-organization, 23
–other differentiation, 88, 138
-psychology, 24, 43
sensorimotor schema, 56, 57
separation anxiety, 35, 116
sequencing, 130
setting, clinical, 4, 24, 33, 46, 51, 52, 55, 63, 66, 71, 92, 99, 141
language of, 61
sexuality, 64, 97, 102, 104, 115, 121
infantile, 4, 11
vs. intimacy, 96
Shakespeare, W., 7
Shuttleworth, J., 8
Sophocles, 7
Southgate, J., 128
Spence, D. P., 68
Spensley, S., 127–128
Spielberg, S., 142
Spillius, E., 136–138
Spitz, R. A., 12, 66
splitting, 95, 105, 106
early, 14
squiggle game, 63
Steele, H., 97
Steele, M., 97
Steiner, J., 133
Steiner, R., xv, xvii, 1–17, 22, 47
Stern, D., *passim*
"still face", 87
stimulus barrier, 24, 60
"strange situation", 87
structural model of mind, 122, 126
structural theory, 104, 121, 122
subjective self, 11
subjectivism, 29, 50, 60
Sullivan, H. S., 25
superego, 121
structure of, and id, 49
symbolic process, verbal, 85
symbolic reality, 65
symbolism, 95
symbolization:
pathology of, 108
and separation anxiety, 35
Symington, J., 101, 102
synchronicity, 96, 130
systematic studies, 109

talking cure, 43, 81
Tallandini-Shallice, M., 99
Target, M., 2
Tavistock, 103, 131, 132, 136
school of baby observation, 8
technical mistake, 135
template(s), 15, 69
dynamic, 98
temporal feeling shape, 57
as paradigm for psychoanalysis, 101
temporality, 4, 7, 127–131
see also: time
tertiary process, 68
"Theo" [Peterfreund], 59
therapeutic knowledge, 25, 29
thing presentation, 34, 95
thinking, 100, 119, 120
absence in, 87
binocular, 95
concept of, 55
infant's, 87
lateral, 104
natural, 120
pathology of, 108
pre-, 57
process, 98
primary, 83
psychoanalytic, 26, 27, 37, 44–47, 51, 63, 75, 109, 112
two-tracked, 105, 106
thirdness, 67
Thom, R., 47, 133, 141

time, concepts of, 7, 82–90, 95, 96, 128–131
  see also: temporality
topographical model of mind, 24, 51, 104, 121, 122, 125
total personality, 49
transference, 25, 34, 63, 68, 89, 96, 115, 122, 130
  –countertransference, 108
transitional object, 12, 34, 65
transitional phenomena, 34, 65
transitional space, 34, 65
traumatized children, 104
Trevarthen, C., 87, 96, 97, 102, 112, 115
Trieb, see: drive
Tronick, E. Z., 87
true self, 129
Tuckett, D., 44, 132–134, 141
Tustin, F., 67

unconscious ego, 8, 121, 122, 126
unconscious ideas, concept of, 48
unconscious meaning, 129
unconscious phantasy, 7, 8, 14, 52, 119
unconscious, the, 17, 25, 33
  and the conscious, 36, 65, 140
  dynamic, 121, 122
  and id, 48, 49
  infantile, 50–51, 93–95
  past and present, 15, 63, 68–69, 89, 97–98
  and research, 26
  specificity of meaning of, 120, 129
  as subject of psychoanalysis, 100, 104
  and time, 128
  use of term, 121–122
undifferentiated phase, 60
University College London (UCL), xvii
unthought known, 89

Varela, F. J., 55
Vaughan, S., 23
Vidal, J.-M., 67
Vienna Psychoanalytic Society, 11
vitality contour, 7, 85, 86, 92, 104, 129
Von Foerster, H., 23, 55

Wall, S., 88
Wallerstein, R. S., xvi, 3, 15, 16, 25, 27–31, 32, 34–37, 44, 65, 67
Wallon, H., 12
Waters, E., 88
weaning phase, 12
Weintrobe, S., 134–136
Widlöcher, D., 98
Winnicott, D. W., 13, 24, 58, 66, 69, 71, 136, 137, 140
  concept of transitional of, 12, 34, 65
  on depressed mothers, 113
  on dreams, 63
  on found and created objects, 53
  on holding, 108
  infant observations of, 12, 79, 129
  influence of on Green, 5
  on play, 120
  on potential space, 141
  on setting, 141
wish-fulfilment, hallucinatory, 60
Wolff, P. H., 42, 43, 45, 48, 54, 56, 58, 59, 66, 77–79, 98
word presentation, 57
work of mourning, 33

Young Adults Research Scheme, Anna Freud Centre, 98

For Product Safety Concerns and Information please contact our EU representative GPSR@taylorandfrancis.com
Taylor & Francis Verlag GmbH, Kaufingerstraße 24, 80331 München, Germany

www.ingramcontent.com/pod-product-compliance
Ingram Content Group UK Ltd.
Pitfield, Milton Keynes, MK11 3LW, UK
UKHW022201190926
475702UK00003B/146

* 9 7 8 0 3 6 7 1 0 5 0 6 8 *